The Open University

Social Sciences : a second level course Urban development Units 27-29

Planning and the city

Prepared by the Course Team

The Open University Press

Cover: Collage of urban renewal components

The Open University Press
Walton Hall Milton Keynes

First published 1973

Designed by the Media Development Group of the Open University

Printed in Great Britain by
COES THE PRINTERS LIMITED
RUSTINGTON SUSSEX

ISBN 0 335 01746 0

This text forms part of an Open University course. The complete list of units in the course
appears at the end of this text.

For general availability of supporting material referred to in this text, please write to the
Director of Marketing, P.O. Box 81, The Open University, Walton Hall,
Milton Keynes MK7 6AA.

Further information on Open University courses may be obtained from the Admissions Office,
The Open University, P.O. Box 48, Walton Hall, Milton Keynes MK7 6AA.

1.1

Block 7   Units 27-29   Contents

Part of block	Set reading	Source of work	Graded reading
Unit 27	1 The optimum size of cities	Course text	1
Unit 28	**Urban renewal**	Course text	1
	1	Set book	1
	2 J. Rothenberg 'Elimination of Blight and Slums' (in Stewart)		
	3 J. Wolpert 'Possible ways of viewing neighborhood change'	Offprint	2
Unit 29	**Planning residential areas**	Course text	1
	1	Set book	1
	2 H. J. Gans 'Planning for people, not buildings' (in Stewart)	Set book	1
	3 M. Rein 'Social planning: the search for legitimacy' (in Stewart)	Set book	2
	4 R. E. Pahl 'Whose city?' (in Stewart)	Set book	2
	5 A. Buttimer 'Community' (in Stewart)		
	6 D. Harvey 'Social processes, spatial form and the redistribution of real income in an urban system' (in Stewart)	Set book	2

Broadcast material for this block is listed separately in Audio-visual Handbook 4

1 Computer-marked assignment
1 Tutor-marked assignment

KEY 1 Wholly relevant to aims and objectives of unit and block
2 Partly relevant to aims and objectives of unit and block, or covering material in correspondence texts in more detail. Selective study is appropriate as indicated in the text

Introduction to Block 7 Planning and the city

In many of the earlier parts of this course there has been discussion of matters closely related to town planning problems. This block concentrates on three problem areas which are, or should be, of concern to every planner. Unit 27 discusses a classic question for which no clear answer has yet been given – is there an optimum size for cities? Unit 28 focuses on an issue which is of rapidly growing importance for nearly every city in the industrialized world – what should be done about the vast legacy of nineteenth century and early twentieth century urbanization which takes the form of what is widely regarded as obsolete building structures and outdated layouts? Unit 29 takes up a theme introduced in Unit 7, which focused on the concept of neighbourhood. Unit 29 examines the planning of residential areas looking at the concept of neighbourhood from the perspective of the planner.

Units 27, 28 and 29 each tackle distinct problem areas and there are no close connections between their subject matter. There are no aims and instructional objectives therefore for the block as a whole. Units 27, 28 and 29 are however closely related to other parts of the course. You should of course give first priority to studying these units themselves. But you should also give some time to relating their content to other parts of the course as specified in the aims and instructional objectives which introduce each unit.

Unit 27 The optimum size of cities
Frank Knox

Part cover: The New York Metropolitan Area, from the Lower Harbour to Fairfield County, Connecticut
Source: Optik Photo: Camera Press

The optimum size of cities

Aims The title of this unit is optimistic. There is little evidence of any optimum size, or even an optimum range of size for cities. Most of the discussion of the factors which ought to influence the size of urban concentrations is of two kinds. There are some criteria which are commonly used to argue that the size of major cities should be limited, and there are some criteria which are commonly used to argue in favour of urban concentrations above a certain size. The aim of this unit is to discuss some of these criteria, and to present some of the relevant evidence to help you form views of your own.

Objectives The unit discusses ten criteria relevant to optimum city size. These are:

Income per head
Relationship of size of major cities to the national population*
Cost of public services
Cost of traffic congestion*
Land and house prices*
Indices of health
Indices of crime
Need for access to countryside*
Desirability of establishing new growth poles*
Desirability of providing a certain level of access to urban facilities to the population outside the major cities
*See 'What you have to do'

The unit analyses the arguments and some of the evidence associated with each of these criteria. You should note that only one of these ten criteria, ie income per head, provides firm evidence in favour of very large cities. Most of the other criteria are usually used in argument against large cities. You are not expected simply to be able to reiterate the points made. But it is expected that, after you have studied the unit, you will be able to:

1 Explain the new concepts introduced in the unit:
   unit cost
   marginal public cost
   threshold size
   growth pole
2 For the ten criteria listed, discuss whether or not these factors are necessarily related to city size.
3 Discuss the possible conflict between the aim of higher income per head and the other criteria.

What you have to do Objective 1 can be achieved through study of the correspondence text alone. The correspondence text also provides sufficient material for you to achieve objectives 2 and 3. But after reading the unit you should look again at material you have already studied which is closely related to these latter two objectives and, if you have time, at other material in the set books. The most relevant parts of the course are:

1 Relationship of size of major cities to the national population: Articles on primate cities and over-urbanization in Breese, and Unit 10, Part 1.
2 Cost of traffic congestion: Unit 17.
3 Land and house prices: Units 14 and 23.
4 Growth poles: Unit 26.
5 Access to the countryside: Blumenfeld (1971).

1 Introduction

The search for a city which is ideal in size as well as in other respects goes back at least to Plato who put the optimum size of a city at 5,040 households, this figure being divisible by all numbers up to twelve except eleven and therefore convenient for tax and other administrative purposes (Plato 1970 p 205). Allowing for dependents and slaves, this would apparently give an optimum total population of between 30,000 and 50,000. Aristotle put it somewhat higher, 40,000 to 60,000. In both cases one of the main considerations was that citizens should have the chance of knowing their rulers individually, and vice versa (Doxiades 1966 p 41). Leonardo da Vinci, described by Lewis Mumford as 'the first advocate of New Towns', proposed to the Duke of Milan that the problems of the existing city of 300,000 should be dealt with by designing ten new towns of 30,000 people each (Mumford 1968 p 202). Sir Thomas More put the population of his Utopia – not all in one city – at 60,000 to 90,000.

In the nineteenth century the problems of the industrial cities gave rise to a number of attempts, especially by the pre-Marxian (or 'utopian') socialists to produce a design for an ideal city, and some practical experiments including those of Robert Owen as well as by private employers at Bournville and Port Sunlight. As mentioned in Unit 26, probably the most important development in thinking on the question of size of towns came at the end of the nineteenth century when Ebenezer Howard put forward his proposal for new towns with populations of about 32,000 each as a solution to many of the most pressing social problems of the time.

Attempts by governments to limit the size of large cities also have a long history. In his book *London – the unique city*, the Danish architect, Steen Eiler Rasmussen has a chapter called 'Attempts to check the growth of London' which recounts that in 1592 an Act of Parliament prohibited the building of any new dwellings within a three mile radius of the existing city of London, and also prohibited any movement of newcomers into existing dwellings within the city. No doubt earlier examples could be found in Britain or in other countries.

In the twentieth century, there are probably few governments which at some time or another have not attempted to check the growth of their capital or other large cities. In the long run, many of these attempts seem to have been ineffective. This has been so even where governments have had close control over economic life and movement of population. In 1931 the Soviet government prohibited the establishment of new industry and other 'town creative' activities in Moscow, and later extended the ban to all towns of over 500,000 population (Balisz 1969 p 207). Despite this the population of the Moscow region grew four-fold between 1926 and 1959 (Balisz 1969 p 201). In 1933 the German government introduced restrictions on the movement of farm workers with the aim, among other things, of reducing the growth of large towns, but these had to be removed after two years (Wunderlich 1961 p 354).

In Britain, since the depression of the 1930s and more particularly since the Second World War, measures to limit the size of London have been enforced, both because of the problems of London itself and also as part of wider national policies aimed at remedying the inbalance in employment growth between the South East and Midlands on the one hand, and the areas of high unemployment – Scotland, Wales, Northern England, South-West England and Northern Ireland. The Barlow Commission (The Royal Commission on the Distribution of the Industrial Population, Cmnd 6153, 1940) recommended:

1 the restriction of the future growth of certain over-large conurbations, especially Greater London;

2 the establishment of a reasonable balance of industrial development between the various regions of the country;

3 the re-development of congested urban areas;

4 deconcentration and dispersal of industries and population from great conurbations.

Defence considerations were one of the reasons for the Commission's recommendation for dispersal and deconcentration, but it was believed that economic and social factors also pointed in the same direction, especially traffic congestion and poor housing in central cities. During the postwar period, it became clear that there was often excess demand for labour in the South East and the Midlands even when nationally there was something like equilibrium in the labour market, and anti-inflation policy became another strand in regional and urban planning. For these reasons the policies initiated in the 1940s have been continued, by measures which include local authority controls on all kinds of building within their areas, industrial development certificates granted by the central government for the establishment or extension of manufacturing establishments, green belts, financial aids to certain regions and to new and extended towns, and other measures.

2 Why bother with city size?

It is not difficult to show that there has been a good deal of inconsistency and some confusion in the idea of the optimum size of a city in the way in which it has actually been used. There has, for example, been as much concern generated about the allegedly excessive size of certain cities as by cities of much larger size at the same period of time. In Britain, the West Midlands conurbation (population 2,446,000 in 1967) has been following a policy of overspill and new town construction though its population is only one-third that of London's. In the Irish Republic, there has probably been as much concern about the size of Dublin (population 735,000 in 1966, about the same as Nottingham's) and its undue 'pull' on the rest of the country as there is in Britain about the dominance of London. In the new towns programme in Britain, there was a gradual increase in the size of population regarded as best for a new town, from between 30,000 and 50,000 when the programme was initiated in 1946 to new cities of a quarter of a million in the early 1960s (including Milton Keynes). The last two examples suggest that the criteria which are in fact being used to say whether a city is 'too large' or the right size are based not so much on the internal characteristics of cities but on their size in relation to the total population of the country, or the rate of growth of total population. In Britain, the number of people who it was expected would have to be accommodated in new towns increased steadily with the sustained increase in the birth rate from 1946 to the early 1960s, and the number of people who it was expected would have to be accommodated in each new town rose accordingly. (Now the expected increase in national population is of course much smaller.)

These criticisms do not dispose of the idea that there is an optimum size at which planners should aim. In fact, it is quite reasonable to view the optimum size as being relative to the total national population rather than an absolute figure, since gravity models in geography indicate that the influence which a town or city exerts is as much a question of its relative as of its absolute size. However once this is recognized, it is clear that ideas of optimum size derived from 'internal' city factors such as the cost of housing, transport and public utilities, and of local government and the provision of social services, cannot in themselves be conclusive.

There is one other important modification, a related one, to the idea of optimum size which must be made at the outset. Taken literally, the idea of an optimum size of city implies that, if it could be discovered, all cities should be of the same size. This is obviously absurd. It is better to have a range of sizes since this allows firms and households a choice as to the size of city in which they want to locate. The size and type of city which will suit one firm will not suit others, and the same probably applies to individuals. A number of geographical theories such as central place theory and the rank-size rule may also suggest the desirability of a range of sizes. (It was suggested in Unit 10, Part I, that these geographical theories do not have any normative implications. This statement may have been rather strong; if it is assumed that existing city size distributions are something like an equilibrium, resulting from maximizing behaviour by firms or households, the theories may have some implications for policy.)

Despite these qualifications, there is a very good reason for studying the question of city size. This is that size is one of the two or three most important questions (with density and location) on which national and local governments cannot avoid taking decisions. At the simplest physical level any local authority in whose area new building is desired – because of population increase or any other reason – must decide which parts of its area are to be built upon and which are not. Nationally, a policy on the distribution of population is needed for much the same reasons. From the more narrowly economic standpoint, overhead investment (housing, communications, public utilities and 'social overhead' investment such as health and education) makes up a large part – in most countries, more than fifty per cent – of total investment, so that any ways in which economies in this investment can be achieved without reducing the quality of the output are likely to be beneficial to the national economy. Specifically, if a particular size of new town or town expansion could be provided more cheaply than others there would be more resources available for other purposes, public or private..

Every decision to impose a Green Belt or otherwise restrict the growth of a city is based on an implicit assumption that the city is too big. If it is decided for one reason or another to restrict the growth of one or more large cities, the question inevitably arises whether this is best done by building or expanding a number of small towns, and if so how many; or a smaller number of larger towns; or one or more large centres as counter-magnets. All these involve decisions about size – though they also involve decisions on other factors such as density, distance from the over-large city and rate of growth of new towns.

City populations in advanced countries are continuing to grow as a result of growth of total populations, and in the developing countries with between forty and seventy per cent of their populations employed in agriculture, urbanization is still in its early stages. Analysis of the past experience of urbanization and examination of the optimum size or size-range of cities could enable the mistakes of the older urbanized areas to be avoided in future city growth.

In most studies of the question of optimum size of towns, and also in this unit, size is considered almost entirely in terms of population size. For some purposes, other aspects of city size – geographical area, total income, total output, employment, imports or exports – may be important. It is pointed out in Section 8 of this unit, dealing with minimum economic size, that a minimum internal market for a given service or production unit can be achieved with a smaller population the higher the *per capita* income. However most of these variables in the short run at least have a fairly constant relation to total population, and if the government wishes to control or influence the size of a particular city, or of cities in general, it can probably do so better by measures affecting the geographical distribution of population and employment than by trying to influence other variables.

3 The concept of optimum size

The idea that there is or may be a size of city which is economically optimum has been developed mainly on the analogy with the idea in economics of the optimum size of firm. This section is devoted to the basic elements of the idea of an economic optimum for the firm or any other type of unit. It makes use of the ideas of average and marginal cost and revenue which you will be familiar with if you have done the Social Science Foundation Course, D100, *Understanding Society*, or the second level course, D222, *Microeconomics*. If you have not done any elementary economics you may find the concepts in this section rather difficult to grasp, but while important they are not very essential to most of the rest of the unit.

The idea of the optimum firm is based on assumptions regarding the shape of the cost and revenue curves, showing how average and marginal costs vary with output. Average costs are, of course, total costs divided by number of units produced; marginal costs are the addition to total costs caused by one additional unit of output. Average and marginal *revenue* are analogous. If 100 units are produced, the average cost might be one pound. However if 101 units are produced, the cost of the 101st unit might be more than one pound – say, £1.1 – in which case the firm is operating under conditions of increasing costs (or decreasing returns). On the other hand it might be less than one pound, if the firm is operating under conditions of decreasing costs (or increasing returns).

Figure 1 City size, costs and revenue

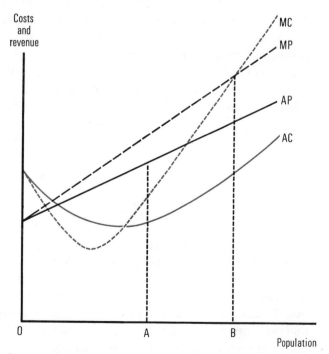

Source: Alonso (1971)

In Figure 1, AC is the average cost curve and MC is the marginal cost curve. The arithmetical relationship between the two is such that when the average cost curve is falling the marginal cost curve is falling more rapidly; when the average cost curve is rising the marginal cost curve is rising more rapidly; and the marginal cost curve cuts the average cost curve at the latter's lowest point. In the case of firms, one of the main reasons why initially there may be decreasing costs is the existence of 'indivisibilities'. For example, a chemical plant or car factory must be a minimum average size to be efficient. Once that size has been reached, a fixed quantity of capital (the factory) may be able to produce more *without* additional plant and buildings, by taking on more labour and buying more raw materials, so that its overhead costs can be spread over a larger amount of output and *average* costs will fall. (The factory and its equipment are known as the 'fixed costs' and the labour and raw materials as 'variable costs'.) A similar situation may apply in the growth of cities. A minimum size may be needed for overhead capital such as electricity, gas, water, schools, hospitals and so on. However in regard to city size, trying to obtain a curve of average costs is obviously much more difficult than with a single firm because of the large number of different industries involved. It may be added that even in the case of individual firms, economists have not found very much evidence of the existence of smooth U-shaped cost curves which are usually assumed in the textbooks. In manufacturing, the cost curve seems to be often L-shaped, ie average costs decline initially as overhead costs are spread over a larger unit of output, and then stay constant for a considerable range of output.

On the revenue side, the curve of the firm's average revenue (ie the price it obtains for its product) and marginal revenue are always assumed to be either horizontal (that is, the price charged does not vary with output) or downward sloping (when the firm has to reduce its price in order to sell a larger quantity). The situation with cities is different; average revenue (in this case, the real wage per inhabitant) may be upward sloping. This means that the marginal revenue curve (the real wages of additional inhabitants) will also be upward sloping, more steeply than the average revenue curve.

Apart from the much greater difficulty of obtaining relevant figures, the most important difference between costs and revenue in connection with cities as opposed to firms is that the former should include public as well as private costs and benefits. (The total of public and private costs or benefits is social costs or benefits.) A public cost or as it is sometimes called an 'external diseconomy', arises when an individual or firm does not bear the full cost of its actions. The usual example of a public cost is smoke from a factory or a house, which results in other houses in the neighbourhood having to spend more money on laundering, etc. These costs could be fairly easily calculated, but others resulting from smoke – the effects on health – while in principle the same, are much more difficult to calculate. Other examples of public costs are noise and traffic congestion. While the idea of a public cost or benefit appears at first sight fairly simple (even though difficult to calculate) on examination it becomes rather elusive and much depends on how widely or narrowly the boundaries are drawn of the entity (firm, industry or area) to which costs or benefits are regarded as 'external' rather than 'internal'. We shall return to this knotty question in Section 6 dealing with traffic congestion. In the meantime we shall assume that public as well as private costs and benefits can be calculated, and that curves can be drawn indicating how social (public as well as private) costs and revenue (or benefits) vary with city size.

Such curves might be as drawn in Figure 1 (Alonso 1971). It is assumed that the cost curve is the traditional U shape. The average and marginal revenue curve is assumed to be upward sloping, meaning that *real* wages are assumed to increase with city size. If the revenue curves were horizontal or downward sloping, the optimum size would of course be smaller.

In the theory of the firm, the optimum size is that at which the firm makes maximum total profits. This is done at the point where the marginal revenue (or, in this case, marginal product) curve intersects the marginal cost curve; in other words, point B on the horizontal scale in the diagram. (If we were talking about the theory of the firm, the horizontal scale would measure output; in connection with city size, it measures population.) To the left of point B on the horizontal scale, every additional unit of output would bring the firm more additional revenue than additional costs, and so would add to total profits. To the right of B, additional units of output would add more to total costs than to total profit, so that it would pay the firm to reduce its output.

Where cities rather than firms are concerned, B is also the optimum size if the criterion is the contribution of the city to total national output. However if it is assumed that the criterion is maximum output (and income) per head of city population (or rather per worker in the city) then A is the optimum size. This is the point at which the distance between the average product and average cost curve is greatest (the slope of the two is equal at this point). Maximum income per head of population is probably a more reasonable aim from the standpoint of an individual city than maximum contribution to national output, though in the theory of the firm it would not be sensible for the firm to stop at this point on the output scale – this would imply maximum profit *per unit of sales*, which presumably is something which no firm wishes to maximize (with the possible exception of consumer co-operatives if they are concerned with maximizing their rate of dividend).

SAQ 1   The following are some hypothetical figures relating marginal cost and marginal real income to city size.

	Marginal private costs	Marginal public costs	Marginal real income (private plus public)
Size group	(£)	(£)	(£)
100,000 and under 250,000	700	200	1,000
250,000 and under 500,000	1,000	200	1,200
500,000 and under 750,000	1,500	200	1,400
750,000 and under 1,000,000	1,700	200	1,600
1,000,000 and under 1,250,000	1,900	200	1,800

According to these figures, what is the optimum size of city in the size-groups quoted if the first of the two criteria above is taken, ie maximum contribution to national output?

For answers to SAQs, see end of unit.

4 Income per head   Whether the aim is maximum contribution to national income, or maximum income per worker in the city, an estimate of the optimum size of city could only be made if detailed information is available on real income for different sizes of cities. (Even this would only measure private, not public, benefit or revenue.) For most countries data on money income per head, let alone real income (ie after allowing for differences in the cost of living) is not available on this basis. However some information is available for the United States, Germany and Japan. This indicates that real income per head of population

or per worker rises steadily with city size. The cost of living is generally higher in large cities, but the difference is not large enough to offset higher money incomes.

In the USA, Fuchs concluded that there is no substantial increase in the cost of living with city size, so that differences in money income reflect differences in real income. This is the most detailed study of the effect of city size on income. His conclusion is that 'standardized hourly earnings in the SMSAs 1,000,000 and over are typically twenty-five to thirty-five per cent higher than in the areas outside SMSAs in the same region, and about fifteen per cent higher than in SMSAs of less than 1,000,000' (Fuchs 1959 p 33). Calculations were made to try to determine how much of this difference might be attributable to differences in colour, age, sex, education, the degree of unionization of the labour force, and the size of employers (which might be an indication of the monopoly power of the employer, and hence of his ability to pay higher wages by raising his price to consumers). The influence of all these factors was found to be small. On the cost of living, Fuchs concluded that 'inter-city differences in cost of living appear to be small in relation to differences in hourly earnings. However, it should be noted that conventional measures of cost of living do not include items like length of time needed to get to work which may vary significantly with city size' (Fuchs 1959 p 34).

Information on Japan and West Germany (quoted in Alonso 1971) also indicate that money income per head of population increases steadily with city size. In Japan mean income per head of population in 1965 was 188,000 yen for the lowest density cities (which are assumed by Alonso to be the smallest) and 340,000 yen for the highest density. In West Germany gross *output* per head for different size-ranges of cities in 1964 rose from 5,400 DM for cities of 20,000–50,000 to 7,500 DM for cities of over 1,000,000.

The fact that money incomes are higher in large cities than in smaller ones is well known and hardly needs detailed statistical evidence. The crucial question is how far the cost of living varies, since money income differences must be deflated by cost of living differences in order to obtain differences in real income. For example, if money incomes per head in city A are 100 per cent higher than in city B but the cost of living is seventy per cent higher, real incomes in A are only thirty per cent higher.

In most countries there is not much information available on how the cost of living differs with city size. It is likely that housing costs are higher, due to higher land prices, and the cost of journey to work will also probably be higher due to greater distances travelled. However at least in Britain in recent years there is evidence that the price of food is lower in large cities, due to the competition of supermarkets, than in small ones. The cost of other items in the consumer's budget such as clothing and household durables may also be less. Fuchs' conclusion that the higher overall cost of living in large cities is not great enough to cancel out the advantages of higher money incomes seems to be applicable to other countries for which evidence is available (Alonso 1971 and Hoch 1972).

The cost of living is likely to differ for different groups of the population. For example, it may be that longer journeys to work (suburbs-to-centre) in large cities apply mainly to white-collar workers, and the journey to work cost for manual workers may not be much greater in large cities. Secondly, statistics may in some ways underestimate the extra cost of living in large cities. Fuchs' point about the omission of the *time* cost to the worker of travel to work from the cost of living applies generally not merely in the US. It is often suggested that external costs imposed on city residents by firms and consumers within the city increase with city size, especially pollution and noise costs. Hoch (1972) says: 'Environmental quality, on net, is likely to deteriorate with increased city size and density. This clearly seems to be the case for air pollution and noise.' I find this conclusion difficult to believe. Noise and air pollution in any area are largely a function of the extent to which the local authority in that area enforces the legislation against these aspects of pollution, and the influence of city size is by comparison minor. In both cases modal split between public and private transport is probably of crucial importance, and large cities are likely to make relatively more use of public transport.

These factors – travel time and pollution costs – are ways in which it is often suggested the real income of inhabitants of large cities may be lower than it seems from figures of income per head deflated by figures of the cost of living. There is another factor, however, which may result in an error in the opposite direction. The inhabitants of large cities may derive a psychic income from the wider range of opportunities open to them in the recreational and related fields. For example, an individual may visit the cinema once a week whether he lives in a large city or a small town perhaps spending the same amount of money per visit (the latter admittedly rather an unlikely assumption) but in a small town his choice of film may be very limited and in the former may be very wide. In these circumstances it is reasonable to suppose that his satisfaction from cinema-going is greater in the large city, and his psychic income greater.

SAQ 2   Of the main components of the cost of living listed below, which three are likely, according to Section 4, to be *lower* in large cities than in smaller towns:
a housing
b travel to work
c fuel and light
d food
e clothing
f consumer durable goods

5 Municipal services and public utilities

In the past, the most usual approach to the problem of the optimum size of city has been to try to find the size for which the cost of providing public services is lowest. Apart from fire and police services and the cost of government itself, the term 'public services' includes two main groups: the social services, including health and education; and public utilities – gas, electricity, water, sewage and telephones. Transport is also sometimes included in public utilities.

There are some serious difficulties in this approach, which would make any conclusions derived from it of very limited use even if only costs and not revenue are being studied.

Probably the most important is the absence in many cases of the lack of any measure of the quality of the 'output'. If it could be assumed that the quality of, say, education and health was the same in all areas of the country, then a low cost of education per pupil, or of health provision per patient or per head of population, would indicate a high efficiency in the provision of the service. In practice, this is obviously not so. Therefore a low expenditure on health and education in one area compared with other areas may mean one of two quite opposite things: that the health and education authorities are providing the service very efficiently, or that they are providing inadequate quantities of the service (in relation to other areas). In principle it should be possible to devise a measure of the output. For example, in health the sickness or mortality rates could be used as an indication of the effectiveness with which the service is being provided; in education the examination results or some other criterion; and in police, the crime rate. Unfortunately such measures are of little value since what is ideally needed is to compare the effectiveness of spending if other factors remain unchanged, and a comparison between areas will be subject to several interfering factors. For example, sickness or mortality rates might be higher in one area than in others because of factors such as climate, pollution or low incomes even though the service provided by the medical authorities was both adequate and efficient.

In public utilities, gas, water, electricity, etc, the product is sufficiently uniform to make it possible to assume that – provided supplies are available at all – quality differences are not very large. In these cases it may be assumed broadly that higher cost per unit of population supplied is an indicator of lower efficiency, and vice versa. Even in the more problematic fields of health, education, police and so on there is some interest in finding out how costs vary between different areas, and whether they are related to population size, provided that the possible differences in the output – the quality of the service – are borne in mind.

There is however another major problem besides that of measuring the quality of the service provided. In local authority services labour costs make up a high proportion of total costs. (This does not apply to public utilities, especially electricity which is very capital-intensive.) Obviously higher wages in a particular city will mean higher wages in the public sector also and hence higher costs of providing public authority services, other things being equal. If this situation exists it is open to several different interpretations. It may be that the most significant aspect is simply the one just stated, that public authorities have to pay higher wages in order to compete with private employers in a high-wage area. In economic theory it is assumed that high wages usually reflect high output, but in this sort of situation high wages in the public sector may or may not do so. There are also two other possible causal relationships if it is found that the cost of providing some or all public services is higher in a high-wage area. The first is that high average incomes may result in a greater demand for the provision of public services, ie the high total or average cost of the latter might be regarded as a result of the income elasticity of demand for public services. The second is that the dominating factor may be that high average incomes mean that more money is available to the city authorities in tax revenue. This will obviously happen if the city authorities impose income or expenditure taxes, but may also happen if (as is usual with local authorities) their tax revenue is made up mainly of property taxes since there may be a connection between high incomes and high property values. In this case – higher incomes making more money available to local authorities through taxation – the causal relationship is quite different from that in the first two possibilities.

Two pioneering studies of how town size may affect municipal expenditure in Britain were made in the 1940s. H. S. Phillips (1942) compared the costs of the main municipal services (elementary education, maternity services, parks, highways, police, public lighting, fire brigade and sewers) taking twelve averages of town size ranging from 56,700 to 697,000 and found that in general the towns with the lowest costs were those with average populations of 124,000 and 211,000. Noting the difficulty of measuring the quality of the service provided he concluded that: 'Towns of below 100,000 inhabitants have little or nothing in their favour, unless it be geographical necessity, but somewhere between 100,000 and 250,000 the evidence, while being too meagre to call for dogmatism, makes it seem probable that town efficiency will have an optimum technical position' (Phillips 1942).

K. S. Lomax (1943) examined expenditure on electricity, gas, water, public transport, education, poor relief, public health, housing and highways for all the county boroughs in England and Wales, broken down into size groups. He concluded that generally both for rate fund services (education, poor relief, public health and housing) and trading services (the remainder) 'with very few exceptions, the largest county boroughs – that is, those whose populations exceed 300,000 – are the most costly to govern' and 'it does appear then that expenditure per head is a function, primarily, of population. This would imply that, in general, as long as the population of a local authority is not above approximately the 100,000 to 150,000 level, the economies of the large unit will operate to keep expenditure per head down, but that above that level the diseconomies will begin to counterbalance the economies and expenditure per head will rise as population increases' (Lomax 1943).

Some more detailed studies have been carried out more recently, mainly in the USA. Probably the most comprehensive study of the effects of town size on municipal expenditure so far made is that by Harvey E. Brazer (1959). Brazer recognizes that to get an idea of how important city size is in influencing municipal expenditure, it is necessary to examine this variable, which is assumed to be *dependent*, not only in relation to city size but also to other *independent* variables. Taking 462 towns in the United States with populations of more than 25,000 people in 1951, Brazer studied the operating expenditure per head of population by city governments in total and in its subcategories of police, fire, highways, recreation and sanitation. (Public utilities – electricity, gas and water – are more frequently provided by private companies than local authorities in the USA.) He related these dependent variables not only to town size but also to six other independent variables: density of population; rate of growth of population; median family income; ratio of city population to metropolitan; employment in manufacturing, trade and services per 100 population (the last two items are intended to give an indication of how far the city is providing services for non-residents, ie commuters and shoppers); and inter-governmental revenue per head of population. This last item – revenue per head of population derived from the Federal or State governments as opposed to the city government – was regarded as possibly significant because 'it is a commonly held belief that government funds are spent with a freer hand when the spending unit is not responsible for their collection' (Brazer 1959 p 22).

The general outcome of Brazer's study was the conclusion that size of town is of negligible importance in determining expenditure per head on any of the items listed, except expenditure on police in which there is a positive correlation with population size though not a very high one (the correlation coefficient is .242).

... Although population size as such is of little consequence, two other variables derived from population data are associated to a substantial degree with per capita expenditures. These are density of population and, for cities for which it has been possible to apply it, the ratio of the city's population to that of the standard metropolitan area in which it is located. There is a clearly observable positive relationship between population density and expenditures with respect to all functional categories except highways, for which the relationship is strongly and consistently negative, and recreation. On the other hand it appears that the smaller the proportion of the metropolitan area's population that is accounted for by the central city, the greater are its per capita outlays. The statistical results obtained tend to substantiate a strong claim to causality for both sets of relationships. (Brazer 1959)

The conclusion that size of town is unimportant is disputed by L. R. Gabler (1969) in a study of the effects of three variables, population size, population density and rate of growth of population. Gabler found that in towns of up to 250,000 population there was no significant relationship with the cost of providing municipal services, except in the case of fire protection, but that in cities above this size 'with the main exceptions of highways and general control, there is a general tendency for the larger cities to spend and employ more per capita . . . Second, there is also evidence to indicate that increased levels of per capita spending are related, at least in part, to city size . . . thus, the evidence suggests that for certain expenditures and/or employment classification in certain states, larger cities do experience diseconomies of scale' (Gabler 1969).

Only one detailed study of the effect of size on local authority costs in Britain has been published since the studies of Phillips and Lomax in the 1940s. This was a study carried out for the Royal Commission on Local Government in England by S. P. Gupta and J. P. Hutton (Royal Commission on Local Government in England, 1968). They considered expenditure by local authorities on housing, health and highways (but not education, the largest item in local authorities' spending). They included all the local authorities in England, but for the purpose of this unit only the County Boroughs and Urban Districts are relevant, not the County Councils and Rural District Councils. (While the County Borough areas usually coincide with fairly self-contained towns, the Urban District Councils may be only one of several making up an urban area, so that the conclusions are more relevant to the size of local government units than to the size of cities.)

In housing, they examined 'costs per foot super' (the total cost of the superstructure of the house) and 'supervision and management costs per dwelling'. The results indicated an inverted U-shaped costs curve, with diseconomies of scale operating up to populations of about 60,000 and economies of scale thereafter. On the health services provided by local authorities (the two most important in expenditure terms being ambulances and home helps) there appeared to be a U-shaped relationship for all the local authorities (rural, urban and county) with the turning point at about 50,000 population, but the authors point out that these conclusions can hardly be applied to County Boroughs since all of these with the exception of Canterbury (pop. 32,000) had populations of more than 50,000. Total expenditure per mile on highway 'maintenance and minor improvements' was taken as an index of efficiency in provision of highway services by local authorities. For County Boroughs there appeared to be an inverted U-shaped curve, with diseconomies of scale (ie costs per mile rising) up to a size of about 104,000 population, and economies of scale after that point.

A number of points made in the study are of general interest. In two instances, housing and (as regards County Boroughs) highways, there appeared to be an inverted U-shaped cost curve, with costs per unit of output rising up to a point and then falling. This is the opposite of the type of cost curve which is assumed to exist in the economic theory of the firm. If the curve is inverted U-shaped, there is no single optimum size. If costs per unit of output are high, if they are near the top of the inverted U, they can be reduced by decreasing as well as increasing the level of output.

One of their findings also illustrates the difficulties in measuring output in the field of local authority services. *A priori*, one would assume that in densely populated areas, where patients probably have smaller distances to travel to hospital, the costs of providing an ambulance service would be less, per patient or per head of population, than in less densely populated areas. The authors found by contrast a significant positive correlation between percentage urban population (they took urban population as a percentage of total population as a measure of density) and expenditure on ambulance service per head. As a probable explanation they suggest 'the greater need and awareness of urban people of the free services'.

Their study also indicates two major difficulties in any study of costs and efficiency, in addition to those mentioned at the beginning of this section. First, local authorities are responsible for only a part of a large and in theory at least integrated service – in health, they are responsible for ambulances, home helps, midwifery and some other minor items but not for general practitioners or hospitals. Obviously the parts of the health service are interrelated; for example, it is conceivable that very numerous and efficient GPs might reduce the need for ambulances to take patients to hospital, alternatively provision of very efficient home care might reduce the need for hospital beds. Examining the efficiency of one aspect of the service may therefore be misleading.

Secondly, as in nearly all studies of local government expenditure only current expenditure by local authorities was considered, not capital expenditure. It is very difficult to obtain meaningful comparisons in capital expenditure.

For one thing, spending on a new fire station or police building may take place only at intervals of twenty, fifty or more years, and on new equipment for the fire and police forces at intervals of say five or ten years. In most local authority accounting, spending is divided into capital and current expenditure (see Unit 20b, 'Financing the City'). Capital expenditure is usually financed by borrowing, and usually requires approval from the central government, while current expenditure is paid for out of the current revenue of the local authority. In the UK this is derived from rates, grants from the central government, and charges for the use of certain services (swimming pools, etc). While the distinction between capital and current expenditure is universal in the accountancy world, it has little justification in terms of economics. To assess economic efficiency, it is necessary to look at total costs, suitably discounted according to the time in which they are incurred. Capital and current expenditures are in some degree substitutable. Other things being equal, it should be possible to reduce current expenditure on the salaries of police, firemen, teachers, etc, by incurring heavy capital costs in the form of expenditure on lavish and up-to-date equipment, and of course conversely. Current costs therefore cannot be considered in isolation, but to include capital costs also would mean that the study would have to cover a long series of years.

Even apart from the basic difficulties, there does not seem to be much agreement between the various studies in the USA and the UK on the optimum size of population for providing local authority services. In public utilities, the significant difference is likely to be between rural and urban areas, not between urban areas of different size. In these, the cost of the distributive network is a considerable proportion of total costs and it is likely to be more expensive to supply a thinly scattered rural population than an urban one. But if attention is confined to the main local authority services – fire, police, water, sewage, and some aspects of health and education – in the USA Gabler has concluded that there are significant diseconomies of scale after the level of 250,000 population is passed, while Brazer concluded that city size has little or no effect on most municipal services. In England, the findings of Gupta and Hutton partly contradict the earlier findings of Lomax and Phillips, who concluded that the optimum size of town is within the range of 100,000 to 200,000 or 250,000 population.

SAQ 3   According to Section 5, in which of the following would you expect the cost per consumer of providing public utility services to be greatest:
a cities of 1 million and upwards
b cities of 250,000 to one million
c towns of less than 250,000
d rural areas

6 Traffic congestion

It has already been mentioned that traffic congestion is one of the main examples of public costs or external diseconomies. This is due to the fact that when an additional vehicle is added to a flow of traffic which is already fairly heavy, the result will be a slowing down of the vehicles already in the traffic flow. Thus if there are 1,000 vehicles in a traffic flow and the addition of another vehicle slows down the existing flow over a length of five miles by one second per mile, the total loss in time is 5,000 seconds. A money value can be placed on this, according to the wages of the people involved. If traffic congestion results in their being late for work and/or losing wages, the loss of wages or output can be used to measure the value of the lost time. Where the travel is for non-work purposes, it is more difficult to measure the value of the time lost, but an arbitrary valuation can still be useful. The newcomer does not pay the cost of the additional loss of time (in fact, any of the vehicles may be regarded as the additional one – there is no reason for discriminating against newcomers). Thus where there is already some congestion, the social (public plus private) costs of traffic are much higher than the private cost. (For a full discussion of social costs in relation to traffic congestion, see Technology Foundation Course, Unit 31, 'The Economics of Traffic Congestion'.)

The marginal social cost of traffic congestion is obviously very relevant to the question of city size. It is safe to assume that most large cities already suffer from some degree of road traffic congestion, so that adding to their population, if the newcomers wish to use cars to the same extent as the existing inhabitants, will add to the congestion. The total losses from delays through congestion will greatly exceed the private costs to the newcomers.

This idea has been used by Dr G. M. Neutze (1966) to calculate the costs from traffic congestion if three towns of widely varying size in the state of New South Wales, Australia, were expanded. His conclusions are striking. He examined Sydney, the capital, with a population of 2,183,000; Wollongong, forty miles away, with a population of 132,000; and the small town of Wagga Wagga, 230 miles from Sydney, which has a population of 20,000. He estimated the effect of a ten per cent rate of growth of population, and assumed that this would result in a ten per cent rate of growth of traffic, in the three places. In Sydney, since all the new growth would take place in the residential suburbs on the periphery, the new residents would have to travel between five and ten miles to get to work, while at Wagga Wagga they would only have to travel one mile. He calculated that a new worker who would cause an increase of 940 vehicle miles in Sydney would cause only 435 in Wollongong and 229 miles in Wagga Wagga. From these figures he estimates the marginal (ie additional) cost through traffic congestion at £32.4 a year in Sydney, £2.0 in Wollongong and £0.1 in Wagga Wagga.

. . . There is thus a saving to the community of about £30 per year for every person who is diverted from Sydney to a centre the size of Wollongong. The saving is only increased by about £2 per year if, instead of to Wollongong, he goes to a centre of about 20,000 population such as Wagga Wagga. (Neutze 1966 p 58)

Since only forty per cent of the population is employed, Neutze estimates that the benefits per *worker* diverted from Sydney to Wollongong are £76 per year, and, if employment in the secondary industries is regarded as 'basic' in the sense that employment in the tertiary industries tends to follow them, since basic industries comprise only forty per cent of the work force, the benefit from diverting a job in basic industry become £152 a year (on the assumption that if one job in basic industry is diverted 1.5 other jobs will follow). While the details of this calculation might be debated, the difference in social cost between an increase in the population of Sydney and in a much smaller town is very large and would seem to provide, as Neutze points out, a strong case for government interference in the location of industry and population so as to divert employment to smaller centres.

It is unfortunate in a unit as lacking in firm conclusions as this one to have to throw doubts on a study which seems to provide definitive figures as guidance to policy, especially when the study relies heavily on economic theory. However some points should be made which may detract from the value of Neutze's calculations. Firstly, even if the costs of congestion can be calculated in this way, alternative methods of avoiding or reducing them should be considered *in addition to diverting employment from large cities to smaller towns*. In particular, where passenger rather than goods traffic is involved, measures have to be considered for diverting traffic from private to public transport – by road pricing and parking charges, or by administrative methods (supplementary licensing for cars entering cities or city centres, restriction of the number of parking places). Common observation does not support the theory that traffic congestion increases in any exact fashion with town size. My experience has been that traffic congestion in London is less than in many smaller cities. This experience may not of course be representative, but it does seem clear that traffic congestion is not more serious in London in proportion to its larger size! It is true of course that the cost of *additional congestion* will be larger in relation to the size of city, but the point is that additional population need not result in additional congestion, given appropriate policy measures. In London a much higher percentage of commuters to central areas travel by rail than in other UK conurbations, which may explain why the state of affairs in London is better, or at least not worse in proportion to its larger size.

Table 1 Travel to work

	Central area workers			All conurbation workers		
	Car	Bus	Rail	Car	Bus	Rail
London	11	19	60	22	24	27
West Midlands	25	60	7	28	40	1
SELNEC	21	59	14	22	43	4
Merseyside	17	58	14	20	48	6
Tyneside	20	62	8	20	49	4
Clydeside	13	61	22	17	55	8

Source : British Road Federation (1971)

Apart from the fact that other methods for dealing with traffic congestion can be devised besides decentralizing employment to smaller towns, there may be a more basic difficulty in Neutze's approach arising from one of the difficulties in the concept of external economies which was mentioned earlier. This is the problem of how to define the unit to which costs (or benefits) are to be regarded as external rather than internal. The costs of traffic congestion are certainly mainly external to the individuals who cause them, which may be a reason for imposing taxes on them, but it could be argued that they are *internal* if the city is regarded as a unit. In Neutze's example, the cost of traffic congestion in Sydney is borne in the main by the inhabitants of Sydney, and it would presumably lead employers and workers to move out if it outweighed the advantages of being in the city and the cost of moving. There may be other factors which justify government intervention in location decisions – such as a high degree of ignorance by both firms and households about costs and benefits in different locations – but it is not certain that the gains from relocation or diversion can be calculated in the way Neutze suggested, or that this kind of calculation is the best foundation for government policies to influence location.

The relationship between traffic problems and city size, and in particular the difficulty of allowing free use of cars in large cities unless they have been specially designed for the purpose, has often been noted. In 1963 the Buchanan Report *Traffic in Towns* concluded after its study of Newbury:

... we think the general lesson is plain enough that it is possible in a town of about 37,000 people, serving a hinterland population of about the same number, to provide for virtually all the use of vehicles that people are likely to want, but it will require drastic and expensive measures on a scale hitherto unexpected for a town of this size. (Ministry of Transport 1963 para 173)

For Leeds (population 500,000) the report concluded on the other hand '... there is no possibility whatsoever in a town of this size and nature, of planning for the level of traffic induced by the unrestricted use of the motor car for the journey to work in conditions of full car ownership.' In 1945, Colin Clark suggested freedom to use cars as one of the criteria for an optimum size of town:

... A size not greatly exceeding 200,000 also appears to be indicated from another aspect, namely traffic and parking. On the assumption (as will be the case in the next generation, and is already the case in the wealthier states of the USA) that nearly every family possesses a car and that a large proportion of the population prefers to drive to work in its own car, it is hard to see how any large city can prevent traffic congestion during the rush hours, or provide adequate parking space in the central business zone. (Clark 1945 p 113)

Thus there seems to be a good deal of agreement that in cities of above 200,000 population it is much more difficult to allow free use of cars than in cities of smaller size, (unless the cities have been specially designed for the purpose). However from this observation two diametrically opposed policy conclusions could be drawn. Colin Clark took the view that because of this cities should be kept small. In the present more environment-conscious era, it would be possible to reverse the argument and say that the impossibility of using cars in large cities, as they have developed historically, is a point in their favour. The same factors – size, density and centralization – which make it difficult to allow free use of cars are also those which make conditions favourable for public transport.

7 Land and house prices

It is well known that house prices and consequently rents are higher in large cities than in smaller towns and rural areas. Of the cost of residential area construction, about seventy-seven per cent is the cost of the dwellings themselves, the rest being costs of site development, roads, sewers and public utility services (Stone 1970 p 197). Of the cost of dwellings, about one-third is the cost of land, and the remainder the cost of building. Construction costs vary from place to place largely as a result of differences in wages in the building industry which are 'less than ten per cent' higher in London than in other parts of England and Wales (Stone 1970 p 114). However most of the geographical variation in house prices is due to differences in land prices, which are systematically related to city size. Naturally, where land prices are high they constitute a larger proportion of total housing cost.

In Britain, London and Birmingham have an influence on land prices much greater than that of other cities. 'The prices of sites with planning consent for residential development vary little from one part of Great Britain to another, except for the conurbations of London and Birmingham and the south coast' (Stone 1970 p 151). Stone's chart of land prices (Unit 14, Figure 2) shows that the price of land per dwelling plot in 1960–4 was between £1,000 and £1,500 within a thirty-to-fifty mile radius of London, and £1,000 to £1,400 within a ten-to-thirty mile radius of Birmingham, while in most other parts of England and Wales it was £500 to £700, ie prices in the areas near London were two or three times as high as in other parts of the country. Land prices are now of course much higher in all areas, but there is no reason to suppose that the *relationship* between the price near London and in areas further afield has changed much. How far the 'sphere of influence' of London should be regarded as stretching is debatable, and the area may be widening. In any case, it is probably much larger than the area within which large-scale commuting takes place. It might some years ago have been regarded as bounded by Ipswich-Oxford-Southampton; with the improvement in communications and especially rail communications it now probably includes Liverpool and Bristol.

The implications of the land price differential, something similar to which is probably found in most countries, are not altogether clear. Many economists hold that land prices are of little importance. This view is taken for example by Richardson: '. . . the high costs of development found in large cities (are) primarily due to high land costs which as a transfer payment rather than a resource cost do not necessarily mean high real costs unless economizing on land in selecting factor coefficients involves higher real costs, eg in the supply of other factors' (Richardson 1972 p 33).

This view is based on the fact that a purchase of land (and of existing, as distinct from new, property) does not lead to any additional demands on the use of the scarce factors of production, labour and capital. The term 'resource cost' in the above quotation means a payment to a factor of production for a service which might not otherwise be performed. Since the quantity of land in existence is fixed, payments made for the purchase of land (by a housebuyer, a builder, a local authority or anyone else) cannot be regarded as on the same footing as other costs; they are, it is argued, only financial and not 'real' costs, ie they only transfer purchasing power from one set of hands to another and are therefore transfer payments. The conclusion that land prices are unimportant from the economic policy standpoint is predicated further on the assumptions that the most important economic problem is the allocation of the scarce factors of production, labour and capital, between competing uses and the (often implicit) assumption that other economic problems can be ignored.

I believe that this line of argument is untenable, and in fact that land price differentials constitute the most important reason for government intervention to control the size of cities. This is because rising land prices are a major cause (as well as being a consequence) of inflation, and of economic inequality. Land price differences may also result in distortions of what might be regarded as an equilibrium geographical distribution of population through the operation of the tax system. Frequently governments have to provide financial aid to offset the effect of high land prices on the operations of local authorities in large cities. The most frequent examples of this are subsidies for public housing and for urban road construction. These are transfer payments, but in effect they constitute a subsidy to the inhabitants of large cities at the expense of the rest of the country and disregarding the question of equity, they presumably have the effect of making these cities larger than they would otherwise be (see also the concluding section of this unit).

8 Minimum economic size

As well as optimum size, minimum size is of considerable importance for planning. In planning a new town or in establishing a 'growth pole' (see Section 9) the question of the minimum population size needed for a town to attain specified objectives is probably more important than the question of what the optimum population is, or at what point population growth should be halted.

In the economics of the firm, it is well known that in many instances especially in manufacturing a minimum scale of output is needed before production is economic (see third paragraph of Section 3). Once this critical minimum size, due usually to the existence of a large fixed capital investment, has been reached, average costs will decline as output increases. The same may apply to many other individual productive units, for example public utilities. For example, in the electricity industry, power stations supplying a large number of consumers can produce electricity much more cheaply than private generators (though these are still used, eg in isolated areas where the national electricity grid does not reach). In addition to minimum economic size, it seems to be true that the unit costs of electricity generation fall steadily as the size of power stations increases. Similarly there may be a minimum economic size, as well as perhaps economies of scale, for hospitals, schools, universities and other institutions. One of the reasons put forward by Colin Clark for regarding a city of about 250,000 people as optimum is that it could be expected to sustain a university of 1,000 to 3,000 students – which he seemed to regard as the optimum, or minimum, number of a university (Clark 1945).

However even if a minimum economic size, or optimum size, for individual 'production' units such as factories, power stations, schools, universities and hospitals could be unambiguously determined, it does not follow that this would have implications for the size of towns (except from the point of view of the number of people *employed by* the unit concerned, as opposed to the number of customers it serves). In the example of a university, there is no obvious reason (from the university's point of view – unless it becomes a matter of national policy that all university students should live at home) why it should draw its students from a single town. It might be true that a minimum number 1,000 to 3,000 students was required for a university, and that the total population needed to produce this number of students was 250,000, but this only implies that towns of this size are desirable if it is further assumed that every town should have a university and that the student population should be drawn entirely from its town.

In fact, universities can draw their students from a wide catchment area. Similarly hospital patients (other than those requiring attention on the spot) can be transported, in the same way as electric power can be supplied to points distant from the producing power station and manufactured goods can be supplied to points distant from the factory. In all these cases, the question is one of balancing the distribution costs involved in supplying wider areas, against the economies of scale which (sometimes) arise from increasing the output of individual productive units. It is doubtful if such factors, varying with methods of distribution as well as methods of production, can provide much general guidance for the planner faced with the need for deciding the size of a particular town.

However in the field of retail and other services, which cannot be transported and which therefore usually involve travel by the customer to the point of sale, the idea of minimum economic size for a town may have a good deal of relevance. In this connection it is useful to link up the idea of minimum economic size with central place theory and the idea of a hierarchy of towns, which you may have encountered in the Social Science Foundation Course, D100, Unit 22 (if you have not, you should read it briefly in conjunction with this part of the present unit). Central place theory assumes among other things that towns can be arranged in a hierarchy and that each 'higher-order' town incorporates all the functions of a 'lower-order' town plus some additional ones. This idea is valuable if the size of towns needed to perform certain functions can be defined; the theory is also valuable in stressing the interrelationship between towns of different orders.

From empirical data it is possible to estimate the size of town needed to provide certain services simply by finding the smallest town in which those services are provided. This approach was used for example in a consultants' report *A New Town in Mid-Wales* (1966), which tried to determine the minimum size of town needed to maintain particular kinds of retail shops, using Census of Distribution data. The method was to find the smallest existing town in which such shops were located, and to assess non-resident shopping in the town by comparing the town's total retail sales with the average retail sales of the region in which it was situated.

Some of the results of the study, which was in the main confined to existing shopping populations of towns in Wales and the Welsh Marches, are shown in Table 2.

Table 2

	Town with lowest 'theoretical shopping population'	Population of town	Population of hinterland
Truform	Birmingham	1,106,000	229,000
Dolcis	Swansea	167,000	54,000
J. Lyons	Shrewsbury	50,000	35,000
Marks and Spencer	Llandudno	18,000	21,000
H. Samuel	Carmarthen	13,000	14,000
Burtons	Ammanford	6,000	5,000
Timothy Whites	Denbigh	8,000	1,000

Source: Economic Associates (1966)

Existing towns serve not only their own populations but that of a hinterland. The size of the hinterland depends mainly on the population of surrounding areas (to assess the strength of which a gravity model was used) and on ease of transport to the towns concerned. The hinterland shopping population for a new town in mid-Wales would be small owing to the thinness of the population. On the basis of the evidence the study concluded:

... There seem to be clear thresholds in the provision of retail and public services in Wales. At one level a minimum threshold shopping population of about 75,000–80,000 will be needed – and that, at Caersws (mid-Wales) will require a population in the town ministering to a hinterland population of only 10,000–15,000. At a lower level but still at a level which supports acceptable urban services, there would still be needed a theoretical shopping population of 30,000 to 40,000, which means a population in the town itself of 15,000–30,000. The two minimal levels of town that are worth working for are 65,000–70,000 and 15,000–30,000. (Economic Associates 1966 para 5.13)

The idea of minimum economic size could also be looked at in terms of *employment* – the size and diversity of employment opportunities and the stability of employment. In the Depression of the 1930s it became clear that it was dangerous for a town or area to be too heavily dependent on one industry or firm, and diversification of employment became one of the ways of dealing with localized unemployment. The aim of a community which is 'balanced' in terms of employment structure and in other ways was laid down for the new towns in Britain, and the New Towns (Reith) Commission was enjoined in its terms of reference to aim at 'self-contained and balanced communities for work and living.' The term 'balance' in relation to employment could be interpreted both in terms of the *markets* of the industries and services in the town, when the object would presumably be to diversify sufficiently to provide safeguards against shifts in demand for the town's 'export' industries or services; and in terms of providing employment opportunities for the different groups of the population – men, women, juvenile workers and perhaps older workers; skilled and unskilled workers; and so on.

Other things being equal, larger towns are presumably likely to have a more diversified employment structure and thus provide both greater opportunities and greater overall stability in employment. One aspect of this is brought out in Moser and Scott (1961, Table 23) which shows that the percentage of women in the labour force is higher in towns of over 500,000 population (36.1 per cent) and towns of 250,000 to 500,000 population (33.7 per cent) than in smaller towns (where it was between 32 and 33 per cent). From the point of view of employers, also, there is a greater choice of labour available in larger towns.

The concept of minimum size might also be given a purely social application – compare this quotation from P. Sargent Florence:

... What size of city is required for a person of certain intellectual interests to have access, at a reasonable cost in time or money, to the satisfaction of a sufficient number of congenial friends? In England educated people are 'choosy' and higher education is intensive rather than extensive. My own experience is that, apart from the special habitat of intellectuals like Oxford or Cambridge, a city of one million is required to give me, say, the twenty or thirty congenial friends I require! (Florence 1955 p 91)

9 Dynamic optima: growth poles and counter-magnets

The approaches to the question of optimum size mentioned so far in this unit have been almost entirely static. Except for the criteria mentioned in Section 8 on 'minimum economic size', they have been used to try to arrive at an optimum population size which would presumably be an upper as well as a lower limit to the population of an ideal town. If national population continued to grow, this would presumably have to be accommodated by building new towns, or expanding those which were below the optimum size.

The idea of optimum size can however be regarded in a more dynamic light. (The student should perhaps be warned here that the words 'static' and 'dynamic' in the social sciences, and especially in economics, have a number of different meanings. Often 'static' is applied by an author to theories he wishes to disparage and 'dynamic' to those he wishes to praise. In this unit, 'dynamic' simply means moving, as opposed to 'static', meaning fixed.) The growth aspect of optimum size may be interpreted in relation to minimizing *construction* costs. This point was touched on in the quotation from the Final Report of the New Towns Committee in 1946, in Unit 26, which pointed out that the availability of labour for construction might be greater in the neighbourhood of existing towns and that this might be an argument in favour of expanding existing towns rather than building new ones.

Apart from an optimum rate of growth from the point of view of the building industry, two concepts have been widely used in which the idea of optimum size has been given a dynamic meaning, in the proposals which have been put forward in a number of countries for 'growth poles' or 'counter-magnets'. The second of these is fairly simple and unambiguous. It means the establishment or enlargement of centres of population and employment which will attract population and employment from areas – often capital cities – which are considered too large. The growth pole idea is extremely vague; as Alonso has said it 'hovers somewhere between intuition and poetry'. It has been given at least two distinct meanings as far as the *purpose* of a growth pole is concerned: patterns of regional growth which will help national economic growth; and growth of certain regions in a way which will promote regional growth and attract industry and population from more congested regions. The latter aim is primarily one of regional rather than national policy; if successfully achieved, it may or may not help national economic growth. It is the latter sense which is relevant here. In this sense it is obviously very similar to the idea of a counter-magnet.

Obviously both the growth pole idea (in its regional policy sense) and the counter-magnet idea involve some implicit or explicit assumptions about the optimum size and/or rate of growth of cities, both in its basic assumption that some cities or areas are too large and also in terms of its assumption about the size (as well as the location and rate of growth) of the towns or areas needed to provide counter-attractions. One of the basic ambiguities of the growth pole idea is the size of the area to which it refers; it has been used to cover all kinds of development (or hoped-for development) from factory estates to city regions. The growth pole idea, however, also contains a number of other theories or assumptions. It has frequently been assumed by proponents of the growth pole idea that there are 'key industries' whose growth will attract other industries or services, though attempts to specify what these industries are have not been very successful. They are often said to be rapidly-growing, science-based industries such as petroleum refining, chemicals, electricity and atomic power; however these are very capital intensive and use only relatively small amounts of labour, so that their impact on the region in which they are situated through the operation of income and employment multipliers is likely to be small.

A full scale discussion of the growth pole idea would take us too far afield from the subject of this unit. The important point here seems to be the link between minimum size and self-sustaining growth. There are almost no examples of a city of 500,000 or more population declining seriously, while there are many examples of cities with lower populations losing population (and of course income, expenditure and employment). This statement might perhaps be contradicted by reference to the experience of some of the US cities, but it is probably better to regard the movement there as taking place within the city from the centre to the suburbs, rather than to outside the city, since the new locations are largely determined by the existing city, and the boundary between the city centre and the suburbs is an historical accident.

The reason why large cities have more power to generate self-sustaining growth is partly a result of their more diversified economic structure. It is also probably a result of the fact that larger cities are more self-contained. Using the classification of export (or basic) and domestic industries developed in Unit 11, it has been suggested that in a town of 10,000 people on the average 68 per cent of sales are 'export' and 32 per cent local; in a town of 270,000 the ratio is 50–50; in a city of 1,707,000 it is 40–60 and in a city region of fifteen million, such as the New York Statistical Metropolitan Area, only 28 per cent of output (services as well as goods) are exported. 'The larger the city, the greater the possibility for economies of scale and thus, the more efficient it is to the extent that it saves transport costs for importing services' (Ullman, Dacey and Brodsky 1971 p 7).

From the standpoint of ability to generate self-sustaining growth, therefore, it seems clear that the balance of advantage lies with large cities. This criterion could come in conflict with others. As mentioned in Section 4, several authors have claimed (though others have disputed) that the optimum size of town from the standpoint of the provisions of local authority services and public utilities is comparatively small, 200,000 to 500,000.

The idea that large cities are needed to offset or reduce the growth of one or more existing large cities also seems plausible in that if this objective is to be attained the counter-magnet city must probably duplicate the facilities, economic, social, cultural and recreational – of existing large cities. (Presumably it is not possible to duplicate the political facilities, since by definition there can only be one capital city, though the capital can be moved.) Where these capital cities are of the size of London, Paris or Tokyo, six to ten million, it may be that the size of any counter-magnet would have to be very large. In countries with smaller total populations and/or smaller capital cities this would of course be less true.

As with the question of minimum economic size discussed in Section 8, there may be a significant difference between developed and developing countries in respect to the size needed to attain self-sustaining growth. This seems plausible on *a priori* grounds because of the larger total population needed to offset lower incomes per head in the latter countries. A UN report discussing the question 'whether there did not exist a critical threshold size which a core region would have to attain in order to achieve self-sustaining economic growth' suggested that: 'in Canada and the United States of America, such a threshold appeared to lie somewhere in the vicinity of 250,000 persons, but in developing countries the size might be nearer to 500,000 or one million inhabitants' (United Nations 1972 para 123).

10 Social indicators: health and crime

Probably the most important complaint about the large industrial cities of the nineteenth century was that they were unhealthy. With the virtual elimination in developed countries of the more serious contagious diseases and improvements in urban environmental conditions the difference between urban and rural death rates is much smaller than it used to be, but there is still a slight differential

Table 3 Standardized mortality rates, 1970 (England and Wales = 100)

	total deaths		conurbations		urban areas of 100,000 outside conurbations		urban areas 50,000–100,000		urban areas under 50,000		rural districts	
	M	F	M	F	M	F	M	F	M	F	M	F
Lung cancer	24,913	5,371	119	120	106	97	99	94	90	90	78	82
Ischaemic heart disease	80,844	58,473	103	99	103	104	99	107	102	104	91	98
Cerebrovascular disease	30,849	48,442	96	95	99	97	102	102	105	106	100	103
Pneumonia	19,164	23,514	117	114	107	98	100	91	88	89	85	96
Bronchitis	21,598	7,338	118	124	107	100	100	97	98	86	74	78
Influenza	3,674	3,576	77	80	102	96	99	100	124	118	111	115
Appendicitis	165	162	106	104	90	77	93	120	92	117	109	79
Suicide	2,271	1,869	108	119	109	95	106	102	92	89	92	81
All causes	293,052	282,141	103	101	103	100	99	99	101	101	90	98

M = Male
F = Female
Source: Registrar-General (1971)

in favour of smaller towns as opposed to large ones, and in favour of rural areas as opposed to urban areas.

In Table 3 some figures are shown from the Registrar-General's *Statistical Review of England and Wales for the Year 1970* which indicate that the standardized mortality rate from deaths from all causes (bottom line of the table) was a few percentage points higher in the conurbations, and in urban areas outside the conurbations with populations of more than 100,000, than in smaller towns and rural districts. The standardized mortality rate (ie the mortality rate after allowing for the influence of the age composition of the population) for each type of locality is expressed as a percentage of the average SMR for England and Wales. An SMR of 105, for example, means that the mortality rate for that area is five per cent greater than for England and Wales as a whole, an SMR of 95 means that it is five per cent less. In the Statistical Review, separate figures are given for males and females and no total of the two is given. This seems reasonable in view of the marked difference between the two in many cases.

A few of the most important causes of death are also shown in Table 3. These figures are a selection from a very long list given in the Registrar-General's Statistical Review. For example, in the Review ten main types of cancer and a category 'other cancer' is listed, but only one type, lung cancer, is shown here. For lung cancer, and bronchitis and pneumonia there seems to be a fairly clear progression from higher mortality rates in large cities to lower ones in smaller towns and rural districts, with the exception that female mortality rates from pneumonia are higher in rural districts than in the first size group of towns, those with populations of less than 50,000. The first two of these diseases might be expected to vary in this fashion due to the effects of atmospheric pollution.

With cerebrovascular diseases (strokes) on the other hand mortality rates in the conurbations and in towns with more than 100,000 people appear to be lower than in other areas. Ischaemic heart disease, one of the most important of the types of heart disease listed in the Registrar-General's Statistical Review, does not appear to show any consistent variation. Appendicitis is responsible for only a small number of deaths but it has been included in the table here as it might be thought that there would be a lower mortality rate from this cause in large towns, where medical facilities are presumably more quickly available. The figures given appear to refute this hypothesis; there appears to be no connection with town size.

A number of qualifications must be borne in mind in looking at these figures. Firstly, they relate only to one year, 1970, and ideally the trend over a number of years should be studied. There may possibly be variations in classification and recording in different areas. However the figures do seem to show that the variations from the national average for England and Wales are in all the diseases quoted, and for the overall mortality rate, quite small, generally a few percentage points each way and in no case exceeding twenty per cent. Indeed the lack of variation as far as mortality rates are concerned might be regarded as more striking than the variation. Also a more detailed examination might show that other factors, such as region or income per head, are more important influences on mortality rates than size of town or the urban–rural distinction. Finally, there has been over the past century or so a considerable reduction in the urban–rural mortality differential and some of the existing differential where large towns appear in an unfavourable light may be due to the after-effects of influences which have been or are being removed. The most important of these is undoubtedly smoke, which is a factor in a variety of causes of death and which since the Clean Air Act of 1956 has been virtually eliminated in those areas where local authorities have made full use of their powers under the Act, most notably in London. (On the other hand, it may turn out that carbon monoxide from motor vehicles is just as lethal – the 1956 Act only deals with *visible* pollutants.)

Suicide is included in the table in that it is important in a different sense, in that it might be regarded as an indicator of the general state of mental health. In this case also there seems to be a positive correlation with size of town, mortality rates from this cause in each size group are generally higher than in those in the next lowest size group, with the exception of female rates in 'urban areas of 100,000 + outside conurbations' which are lower than those in 'urban areas 50,000–100,000'; and male rates in 'urban areas under 50,000' and 'rural districts', for which the figure is the same. Here also it might be that factors other than city size, including location within cities, are as important, or more important.

In a separate table the Registrar-General shows infant deaths, ie deaths of babies under one year old, though these are not expressed as a percentage of the national average. Infant mortality rates (deaths per 1,000 live births) show a definite though not very large association with city size. In 1970 the infant mortality rate in the conurbations was 19.97, in 'urban areas of 100,000 + outside conurbations' it was 19.18, in cities of 50,000–100,000 it was 17.30 and in rural districts 15.98. (Registrar-General 1971, Part 1, Medical Tables, Table 24).

When we turn from health to crime, there is again an obvious link – more marked than in health – with city size, and also a differential in favour of rural areas as opposed to urban areas (Table 4). As with health, there are difficulties in classification and recording which have to be borne in mind – it might be, for example, that in rural areas certain offences are more likely to be dealt with by a caution from the police than similar ones in cities, though this would seem improbable for the more serious types of crime. Table 4 shows that in 1965 total crimes per 100,000 population were roughly fifty per cent more numerous in the very large towns of England and Wales than in the small towns, and more than twice as numerous in the largest towns as in the areas covered by 'County Forces'. (The 'six very large towns' in the table are Manchester, Liverpool, Birmingham, Bristol, Sheffield and Leeds.) The three right-hand columns of the table show crime rates for indictable offences. These are regarded as the more serious types of crime, generally tried by a judge and

Table 4 Crime, England and Wales

Police area	Crimes per 100,000 population		Major crimes per 100,000 population, 1965		
	1955	1965	offences against the person	breaking offences and robbery	larcenies
London (Metropolitan Police District and City)	1,171	3,378	9	434	1,122
Six very large towns	1,401	3,327	17	473	646
Eleven large towns	1,120	3,333	9	358	499
Twenty-nine medium-size towns	968	2,795	5	302	434
Twenty-seven small towns	1,047	2,544	5	229	350
Total: Urban forces	1,160	3,176			
Six very large counties	872	1,835	4	244	311
Seventeen large counties	834	1,670	4	195	298
Seventeen medium-size counties	793	1,770	5	176	289
Ten small counties	645	1,719	5	147	266
Total: County forces	830	1,747			
Total: England and Wales	989	2,374			

Source: McClintock and Avison (1968)

jury after formal indictment, as opposed to summary convictions which are handed out by magistrates. It appears that crime rates for all three of the main categories of major crimes, 'offences against the person', 'breaking offences and robbery', and 'larceny' are more frequent in relation to population in large towns than in small ones or in country areas, with the exception that London had smaller rates in 1965 for the first two of these types of offence than did the 'six very large towns'. Generally the incidence of these major crimes is two or three times as great in large cities as in small towns and country districts.

This relationship also exists in the USA:

... The total crime index rate in large metropolitan areas (1,782 per 100,000) is nearly two times higher than the rate in other cities (996) and about three times the rate in rural areas (568) ... when crime rates are examined by groups of cities of decreasing size, the constancy of decreasing rates is especially striking. (Wolfgang in Wilson 1968 p 8)

These figures are of course open to several different interpretations as regards causal relationships. The most frequent form of crime is theft and one possibility might be that, if there is more valuable property (per head of population) in large cities, the geographical incidence of crime is determined by the location of its targets. Another possibility is that individuals with criminal tendencies migrate to cities, for one or more reasons such as the location of their targets and possibly the lower risk of detection. The implication of this might be that if they did not carry on their activities in large cities – if for example the average size of large cities was reduced – they would do so somewhere else. However there is some evidence that the relationship of city size to crime rates is more fundamental, and may to some extent be a causal one. If crime rates are taken in proportion to people *born* in different areas, ie if migration is disregarded, city populations still appear in an unfavourable light. This has been found in the USA, and

... Recent data for Norway and Denmark are also suggestive of the criminogenic (ie producing crime or criminality) character of cities. Christen reported that, of all males born in Norway in 1933, five per cent were registered as offenders by 1958. Nine per cent of males from the big city of Oslo became offenders, compared with eight per cent from other areas and four per cent from rural areas. Wolfgang examined a sample of over 1,000 males in Denmark who were twenty-one years of age or older in 1953–4, and found that 9.6 per cent were offenders; thirteen per cent lived in Copenhagen, nine per cent lived in towns of between 2,000 and 19,000 inhabitants, and only six per cent lived in small towns with under 2,000 inhabitants. (Wolfgang in Wilson 1968 p 250)

11 Conclusion

The seven criteria (corresponding to section headings four to ten inclusive) which have been discussed are probably the most widely used in discussions of the optimum size of cities. It has been thought useful to consider a limited number of the more important criteria in some detail rather than try to cover as many criteria as possible. However a much longer list of criteria could be given. O. D. Duncan (1957) lists ten criteria: physical size of city ('the theorist of optimum city-size, demands that cities be small enough to enable ready access to the countryside and a reasonably moderate journey to work'); health; public safety; municipal efficiency; education and communications; public recreation; retail facilities; number of churches and voluntary associations; family life (under which Duncan considers the proportion of the population which is married, the birth rate, and housing standards); and 'miscellaneous psychological and social characteristics of urban life', including the role of cities in diffusing innovations.

Even if sufficient information were available to lay down a precise optimum for any one of these criteria considered singly, the problem of *weighting* the different criteria to arrive at an overall or synthetic optimum would still pose serious, probably insoluble, problems. For example, there is evidence that while there are economic advantages in large cities (especially higher real income per head) there are social factors, especially the crime rate, which point to the desirability of cities being as small as possible, and indeed to the superiority of rural over urban life.

To make any progress on this matter, it would be necessary to look at a number of different ways – including a reduction in the size of cities – for trying to deal with crime. Most of those who have proposed an explicit or implicit idea of an optimum size of town have been concerned with this as a means to an end, not as an end in itself. They have done so because they have regarded size of town as an important factor influencing the housing problem, traffic congestion, health, crime, and so on. However influencing the size of cities is obviously only one way of trying to deal with these problems, and if any one of them is being considered in detail, consideration of the merits and demerits of different policies is more important than trying to arrive at an optimum size of town.

Today, probably the most important single reason which is usually suggested for limiting the size of cities is traffic congestion. However, traffic congestion can be dealt with by means other than limiting the size of cities – by changing the internal structure of the city (decentralizing employment from central areas to the outskirts if traffic congestion is mainly due to the concentration of employment in central areas), or by road pricing, administrative restrictions on the use of cars, or staggering of working hours.

In the past, one reason put forward by social reformers and proponents of new towns was a rather vague social one, to the effect that inhabitants of large cities suffer a loss of community feeling (see Unit 26). More detailed studies of particular localities in cities, such as the famous study of East London by Peter Wilmott and Michael Young, have cast doubt on this. In any case, insofar as community feeling can be created by deliberate planning – which is extremely doubtful – it can probably be done as well by measures affecting the internal structure of cities as by measures affecting their size.

A key factor in the views of the advocates of new towns and limiting the size of large cities in the past was that of maintaining access to the countryside. This was apparently regarded as an end in itself by some social reformers, but by others was a subsidiary aim viewed as a means of improving the health of the population and providing them with better recreational facilities. As far as the health objective is concerned, the reduction in the rural–urban mortality and morbidity (sickness) differential would seem to have made this objective rather superfluous.

The aim of maintaining access to the countryside was put forward at a time when total national, and urban, populations were much smaller than at present. It has to be considered now whether this aim should not be subordinated to the aim of preserving some countryside, especially of high scenic value, an objective which might be better attained by restricting the spread of urban areas in certain directions rather than by limiting their total size. In the case of London, for example, this might mean preventing any further extension southwards into Kent, Sussex and Hampshire even if this meant considerable extension in some northwards and eastwards directions. The same geographical desiderata might be put forward for the West Midlands conurbation.

Another important related objective was minimizing journey to work. This is perhaps a more valid reason for limiting the size of large cities, but here, as mentioned in discussing traffic congestion, it can probably be done as well by measures affecting the internal structure of cities as by measures affecting their total size. However the journey to work question is closely related to the question of housing prices and rents. This may be a more important and valid reason for limiting city size. Both problems are related to city size and to each other. As you will be aware from the sections in Unit 23 dealing with density and land price gradients, for a person working in a city centre there is a fairly rigid trade-off between transport and housing costs. A household can minimize its travel to work costs by living near the city centre, but will have to pay high rents or house prices; or it can obtain better and cheaper accommodation by living farther away. For this reason the housing and urban transport problems cannot be considered in isolation, and decentralizing employment from city centres to the outskirts should help towards a solution of both. (This statement should perhaps be accompanied by a qualification that in the UK suburbanization is not accompanied by development at very low densities, such as has happened in the USA, which has the effect among other things of leading to a decline in public transport.)

If housing prices and transport costs are directly related to city size, limiting the size of large cities would be one of a number of possible measures for dealing with both. However as regards land prices, two qualifying points need to be borne in mind. Large cities influence land prices over a wide area, as shown by the figures for London and Birmingham quoted in Section 7, so that reducing them may be a question of regional planning as of planning affecting the size of particular cities. Also, much the larger part of the recent rise in land prices in most countries has been due to inflation, since purchase of land and property is one of the best hedges against inflation, and is only to a minor extent the result of 'real' factors such as growth of population and growth of income per head. (In the period of the most rapid rise in land prices in Britain since about 1969, population and income per head have in fact both been growing *less* rapidly than in most of the postwar period.) In the UK, entry into the EEC has also been an important factor as regards the price of farm land.

In dealing with any of the policy problems mentioned in this unit, it is clear therefore that controlling city size is only one of several policy measures available for dealing with them, and in most cases one of the least important policy measures. But the idea of optimum size may nevertheless still be of value. It should, given adequate research, be possible to link the results of studies of optimum size with the results of other lines of enquiry. Rather than asking 'What is the optimum size for a city?' we might ask 'Are there factors tending to make cities larger than they would otherwise be?'

One of the most important of such factors may be the effect of government activities on the geographical distribution of population and employment. Some of these, such as the Regional Employment Premium and farm subsidies, are deliberate. Others are not, and the geographical effects are generally not taken into consideration when the decisions are being made. Among these government activities with largely unintentional effects on city size as well as on other aspects of location are grants made by central government to local authorities for certain purposes. Before 1967, for example, 75 per cent of the cost of Class 1 motorways (which category includes urban motorways) were paid for by the central government, with decreasing percentages for lower grades of road. (Since 1967 the percentage of the cost of urban motorways and other principal roads is still 75 per cent, but grants for non-principal roads are made through non-specific grants.) This presumably constitutes a considerable subsidy to large cities, or at least to those which engage in large scale urban motorway construction, at the expense of the rest of the country. If public transport in large cities is subsidized by *central* government, the effect is the same. From this point of view – maintaining something like an equilibrium in the geographical distribution of population – such subsidies should be paid for by local authorities rather than by the central government. Other government grants to local authorities, such as those calculated on a social needs basis, may have the same effect.

There are a number of subsidies in the opposite direction, from urban to rural areas, including farm subsidies and the internal subsidy (ie not through the government) given by the electricity industry to rural at the expense of urban electricity consumers. Only detailed research would show whether *per head of population* these outweigh the subsidies to cities, and which cities and size-groups of cities benefit most from the operation of central and local government fiscal operation.

SAQ 4   Which of the following did G. M. Neutze take to estimate the marginal social cost of traffic congestion in a large city:
a average time taken in travel to work;
b average distance travelled to work;
c average fare paid per person in travelling to work;
d the cost of additional traffic delay caused by an addition of one person to the city's population;
e cost per mile of building urban motorways.

SAQ 5   Which of the following is a valid reason why the minimum economic size of a city in a developing country is likely to be larger than in a developed country?
a Average size of the industrial unit is likely to be smaller in a developing country.
b Exports to other countries are likely to be a larger proportion of output in developing countries.
c Income per head is likely to be higher in developed countries.
d Costs of construction are likely to be lower in developing countries.

SAQ 6   Which of the following rates, according to Section 10, are positively correlated with city size, ie they increase as city size increases:
a lung cancer
b heart disease
c bronchitis
d appendicitis
e suicide
f all crimes
g major crimes

Answers to SAQs

Answer SAQ 1   250,000 and under 500,000

Answer SAQ 2   d, e, and f

Answer SAQ 3   d

Answer SAQ 4   d

Answer SAQ 5   c

Answer SAQ 6   a, c, e, f, g

References   ALONSO, W. (1971) 'The economics of urban size', *Papers and Proceedings of the Regional Science Association*.

BALISZ, B. (1969) *Physical planning for the development of new towns*, New York, United Nations.

BLUMENFELD, H. (1971) *The Modern Metropolis*, Cambridge, Mass., MIT Press (set book).

BRAZER, H. E. (1959) *City expenditures in the United States*, National Bureau of Economic Research, Occasional Paper No 66, New York.

BRITISH ROAD FEDERATION (1971) *Traffic in the conurbations*, a study by Alan M. Voorhees and Associates, London.

CLARK, C. (1945) 'The economic functions of a city in relation to its size', *Econometrica*, April, pp 97–113.

DOXIADES, C. A. (1966) *Between Dystopia and Utopia*, Hartford, Connecticut, Trinity College Press.

DUNCAN, O. D. (1957) 'Optimum size of towns' in HATT, P. K. and REISS, A. J., *Cities and Society*, Illinois, Free Press of Glencoe.

ECONOMIC ASSOCIATES (1966) *A new town in mid-Wales – consultants' proposals*, London, HMSO.

FLORENCE, P. S. (1955) 'Economic efficiency in the metropolis' in FISHER, R. M. (ed) *The Metropolis in Modern Life*, New York, Doubleday and Co.

FUCHS, V. R. (1959) *Differentials in hourly earnings by region and city size*, National Bureau of Economic Research Occasional Paper No 101, New York.

GABLER, L. R. (1969) 'Economies and diseconomies of scale in urban public services', *Land Economics*, November, pp 425–34.

HOCH, I. (1972) 'Income and city size', *Urban Studies*, June 9, 3, pp 299–328.

LOMAX, K. S. (1943) 'Relationship between expenditure per head and size of population in county boroughs in England and Wales', *Journal of the Royal Statistical Society*, 106, Part 1, pp 51–9.

MCCLINTOCK, F. H. and AVISON, N. H. (1968) *Crime in England and Wales*, London, Heinemann.

MINISTRY OF TRANSPORT (1963) *Traffic in Towns*, London, HMSO (The Buchanan Report).

MOSER, C. A. and SCOTT, W. (1961) *British Towns: A statistical study of their social and economic differences*, Edinburgh, Oliver and Boyd.

MUMFORD, L. (1968) *The Urban Prospect*, London, Secker and Warburg.

NEUTZE, G. M. (1966) *Economic Policy and the Size of Cities*, Canberra, Australian National University Press.

OSBORN, F. J. (1934) *Transport, Town Development and Territorial Planning of Industry*, New Fabian Research Series, No 20.

PHILLIPS, H. S. (1942) 'Municipal efficiency and town size', *Journal of the Town Planning Institute*, 27, May–June, pp 139–48.

PLATO (1970) *The Laws*, Harmondsworth, Penguin Books.

RASMUSSEN, S. E. (1962) *London – the Unique City*, Harmondsworth, Penguin Books.

REGISTRAR-GENERAL (1971) *Statistical Review of England and Wales for the year 1970*, London, HMSO.

RICHARDSON, H. W. (1972) 'Optimality in city size, systems of cities and urban policy: a sceptic's view', *Urban Studies*, October.

ROYAL COMMISSION ON LOCAL GOVERNMENT IN ENGLAND (1968) *Economies of scale in local government services*, Report by S. P. GUPTA and J. P. HUTTON, London, HMSO.

STONE, P. A. (1970) *Urban Development – Standards, Costs and Resources, 1960–2000*, Cambridge University Press and National Institute of Economic and Social Research.

ULLMAN, E. L. and DACEY, M. F. (1960) 'The minimum requirements approach to the urban economic base', *Papers and Proceedings of the Regional Science Association*, pp 175–94.

ULLMAN, E. L., DACEY, E. F. and BRODSKY, H. (1971) *The Economic Base of American Cities: profiles for the 101 Metropolitan areas over 250,000 population based on minimum requirements for 1960*, Seattle, Centre for Urban and Regional Research, University of Washington.

UNITED NATIONS DEPARTMENT OF ECONOMIC AND SOCIAL AFFAIRS (1967) *Planning of Metropolitan Areas and New Towns*, New York, United Nations.

UNITED NATIONS ECONOMIC AND SOCIAL COUNCIL (1972) *Report of the Interregional Seminar on the Financing of Housing and Urban Development*, New York, United Nations. (Report of seminar held in Copenhagen 25 May–10 June 1970.)

WOLFGANG, M. E. (1968) 'Urban crime', in WILSON, J. Q. (ed) *The Metropolitan Enigma – inquiry into the nature and dimensions of America's 'urban crisis'*, Harvard University Press.

WUNDERLICH, FRIEDA (1961) *Farm Labour in Germany, 1810–1945*, Princeton University Press.

Acknowledgements

Grateful acknowledgement is made to the following sources for material used in this unit:

Figure 1: Regional Science Association for W. Alonso, 'The Economics of Urban Size' in *Papers of the Regional Science Association* XXVI, 1971; *Table 1:* British Road Federation and Colin Buchanan and Partners for *The Conurbations*; *Table 2:* The Controller HMSO for *A New Town in Mid-Wales – Consultants' Proposals*, 1966; *Table 3:* The Controller HMSO for *The Registrar-General's Statistical Review of England and Wales 1970, Part 1, Medical Tables*; *Table 4:* Heinemann Educational Books Ltd for F. W. McClintock and N. H. Avison, *Crime in England and Wales*, based on data extracted from 'Supplementary criminal statistics for England and Wales', 1955 and 1965.

Unit 28 Urban renewal

Brian Clarke
Lecturer, University of East Anglia

AYLMER
TOWER

Part cover: High rise development in Norwich

Introduction It would appear from reading newspapers or listening to the radio and TV that the city is suffering a general malaise. Problems, such as poverty, poor housing, poor and fallible services, social and racial tensions are being continually brought to our attention. At one moment we are shown empty office or administrative buildings, at another overcrowded tenements, and at another cleared and apparently bomb devastated areas waiting. One sees the homeless or underprivileged complaining of their lack of opportunity, the tenant unable or unwilling to improve living conditions, the owner regretting that public policy has made property ownership a liability rather than an asset, the developer in a position where non-occupation may be as profitable as occupation, the councillor pleading that demands are exceeding the ability of city government to cope, and the planner arguing that people are never satisfied. Where plans, policies or palliatives are suggested and implemented it appears that problems increase rather than decrease.

Yet in spite of everything the city is still the centre of human civilization. It is to cities that migrants move, and it is in cities that all sections of society search for places to live and work. It must be admitted though that over time cities would seem to suffer from a variety of problems, and these reflect both the stage that the city community has reached in its development and also the general state of society at the time. Some specific problems are shown in economic, some in social and some in psychological form. However, they are all part of the general process by which city communities function and intereact.

Concern over the city is not new. J. Strong wrote in 1885:

... Few who will read these pages have any conception of what these pestilential human rookeries are, where tens of thousands are crowded together amidst horrors which call to mind what we have heard of the middle passage of the slave-ship. To get into them you have to penetrate courts reeking with poisonous and malodorous gases, arising from accumulations of sewage and refuse scattered in all directions, and often flowing beneath your feet; courts, many of them which the sun never penetrates, which are never visited by a breath of fresh air. You have to ascend rotten staircases, grope your way along dark and filthy passages swarming with vermin. Then, if you are not driven back by the intolerable stench, you may gain admittance to the dens in which these thousands of beings herd together. Eight feet square! That is about the average size of many of these rooms. Walls and ceiling are black with the accretions of filth ... These are men and women who lie and die, day by day, in their wretched single room, sharing all the family trouble, enduring the hunger and the cold, and waiting, without hope, without a single ray of comfort, until God curtains their staring eyes with the merciful film of death. (Strong 1885)

J. Habberton four years later commented:

The amount of suffering that exists in all large cities merely through enforced conditions of life passes power of expression. No one has ever yet been able to do the subject justice. Many who have worked among the poor have lost life and hope, and mind itself, in contemplation of the suffering and sorrow which they have witnessed and been unable to relieve. To attempt to care for the poor of a large city affects one very much like an effort to pour water into a sieve; the demand is continual, yet nothing seems to be effected. (Habberton 1889)

What is new is an increased public awareness of the problems facing the city, and a feeling that these problems need to be solved if society, as we know it, is to continue to function. That is to say, it is becoming felt that the scale of urban problems has increased so much that they are threatening the city itself.

Different problems have been described elsewhere in this course. For example, John Collins in Unit 25 has shown in his analysis of the shanty town the way in which continued citybound migration poses intense problems both for the migrants, and for existing inhabitants and government. David Boswell in Unit 9 in his description of social segregation and the slum has shown the impact of sectoral isolation within the city. But one major problem not so far analysed is the decay of the physical fabric of the city over time, and this theme provides the basis of this unit.

Aims

The aims of this unit are to discuss primarily in relation to the residential areas of the city:

1 The nature of the problems created by changes in housing standards, tastes and aspirations for residential areas where the housing stock is old and outdated.

2 The consequences of governmental action in such areas, especially when this action results in renewal or rehabilitation.

From personal experience you must be aware of the ways in which urban areas physically change as they age. Reflecting changing tastes and aspirations areas within the city become more or less attractive. In some areas government has taken a direct hand in encouraging change by demolition and rebuilding, or by providing funds to allow people structurally to improve buildings and services. It is the intention of this unit to attempt *to consider* the need for the alternatives, and the consequences of various alternatives in *urban renewal*. This will be done mainly in *economic terms*, since purely social consequences of urban change and renewal are discussed elsewhere.

You will also find that there is a concentration upon renewal and redevelopment problems in Britain. This is partly because Britain is in many ways an ideal case study for the types of problems that are facing, or will face other urbanized nations. As will be shown, most of urban decay problems result from change over time, and the longer the time that has elapsed since development took place the greater is the probability that renewal is taking place, or is needed. Since Britain led the Industrial Revolution, and since it urbanized first, then its problems have reached the most advanced stage.

You should also remember that although the economic and social forces promoting change affect all land uses, the predominant land use within the city is residential. That is to say whilst there are many renewal and redevelopment problems for industry, offices and shops, these land uses account for only a small proportion of the total urban area. It is those problems and policies that affect residential areas that have the greatest economic, social, psychological and spatial impacts. For this reason most research work has, probably rightly, tended to *concentrate on homes and people*, and is why there is a similar concentration in this unit.

Objectives

After studying the correspondence text and the specified reading you should be able to discuss the general *process* of decay renewal and:

1 List ways in which *property values change* after initial construction has been completed.

2 List ways in which older residential areas become economically and *socially outdated*.

3 Explain in your own words what is usually meant by:
blight
compulsory purchase
filtering
ripe for development

> slum
> unfit dwelling
> comprehensive redevelopment
> urban rehabilitation

4 Describe the nature of those factors modifying the free operation of market forces within the market for land and property in older residential areas.

5 Describe the nature of costs and benefits to those involved in urban renewal and rehabilitation schemes.

6 Describe the policy alternatives open to governmental bodies with respect to older residential areas.

7 Discuss the housing problems facing members of lower income groups and the effects that urban renewal and rehabilitation schemes are likely to have.

What you have to do

This unit is not written around any individual article or reference. This means that you should be able to achieve a general understanding of the objectives from the main text. At various stages in your reading of the text, however, you might find it interesting to look at additional material.

Objective 1 is fairly straightforward. Thomas (Unit 11) describes the general process by which land is developed, and also provides a useful terminology. But you should note that Thomas is describing the factors which determine land values at a particular point of time, and not, as analysed in this text, the way in which land values change as buildings age.

Objective 2 is fairly well touched on in the text. You might perhaps find it useful to list a set of life style changes that are reflected in building standards and compare these with the listing in the text.

Objective 3 is probably best achieved through the use of the correspondence text, and then by comparing the definitions used within it with those suggested in J. Rothenberg, 'Elimination of Blight and Slums' in M. Stewart (ed) (1972) The City, pp 130–54. You should be careful to note that though the various definitions are listed separately under this objective they are in fact very closely related, and that the definitions of one, eg ripe for development, will affect others, eg planning blight.

To meet objective 4 you could perhaps refer back to Rothenberg, when he is discussing internal and external costs. You will probably also find it useful to put yourself into the position of an inner city property owner trying to improve his property with limited capital and to list the parts of the process that you would have to go through to obtain backing and permission to change your property. You could also find it worthwhile though not essential to look at the Wolpert paper, 'Possible ways of viewing neighbourhood change' reprinted in Supplementary Material.

Objective 5 is a difficult objective to understand, not because of any difficult concepts, but because of the difficulty of comparing economic costs and benefits with their social equivalents. Probably the best way of doing this is to list the various people involved in a renewal project, using the text, and then to list simply as factors, the costs and benefits falling on each. Only then should you try to put value judgements upon their importance.

Objective 6 is fairly straightforward. But it is important for you to remember that the policy alternatives each contain subdivisions, and that you are really dealing with a continuum rather than a set of discrete opportunities. You should also note how an inner city policy has implications upon general urban development policy as a whole. This is stressed in the text. Finally you need to remember that whilst all policies are potentially open to government, in practice their usefulness is constrained by a whole series of external factors, such as grants or finance.

When looking at objective 7 you will find it useful to refer to either Rothenberg, or to Wolpert in their discussions of the social costs imposed on the lower income groups in any redevelopment scheme. Remember that the points made in relation to objective 5 are also important here.

You will see that objectives 1–4 are fairly straightforward and descriptive. You should be able to isolate the main points fairly easily. It is important to remember though, that the definitions you use here are of importance both in your general understanding of this unit, and also may be of considerable importance in the real world process of urban renewal. Objectives 5, 6 and 7 are a little more complicated since they involve you in trying to value both social and economic costs. It is possible to take a value orientated, or political, stance on these questions. If you do this prior to tackling the problem of social and economic inequalities it is likely that your opinion may become reinforced, rather than a general understanding obtained. Perhaps the best way of gaining a general insight is to take the role of the different people within the process when you have finished reading the unit, and try to understand their separate problems from a neutral viewpoint.

1 Site and property values

Once land has been converted from agricultural to urban use the development process has not been completed. Those social and economic forces that determine the particular type of conversion (to residential, industrial or commercial development) are not static, ie they change in time. Such changes mean that the suitability of an area for a particular land use is continuously changing. At the same time buildings become out of date as the tastes and aspirations of users change.

In Unit 14 you will have looked at the factors that determine the initial type of development, and you might perhaps find it worthwhile to refer to this unit now. In summary these factors fall into two groups – internal and external. The former includes, for example, drainage and elevation, the latter accessibility, ie the accessibility of the site to others of interest to the potential user. If one accepts that accessibility will vary over time, for example through changes in communications or through the change of use of other sites within the city, then one can infer that the site value of any particular site is continuously changing.

The value of any particular building, once constructed, will depend not only on these site factors but also on costs unique to the building itself, such as rates, structural maintenance costs, depreciation, wear and tear. The relationship between these two values, ie the value of the land and of the buildings reflecting general socio-economic factors will determine not only when or whether redevelopment or renewal is possible but also plays a part in controlling how it takes place.

Once a building has been constructed on a piece of land then the developer can expect his return from this building to change with time. A continuous cycle of change affects all buildings. Initially the building may increase in value (if demand for this particular type of building exceeds supply). This is then followed by a long period of maintenance and depreciation on the structure until it becomes necessary or worthwhile for the owner to demolish and rebuild. Of course this gradual decline may be halted, or modified for a while, by internal alterations or by maintaining a good structural condition.

'At any period of time the value of the building will be a function of the stream of net benefits to any future owner' (Goodall 1972). If the site value remains static, that is to say there are no major supply/demand changes for land in this particular situation, then the economic life of a building will be much as in Figure 1.

Here the site value of the building is assumed to be static and the line VV is thus horizontal. The depreciation of the building or property over time is shown by the line PP. In Figure 1 you will note that no allowance has been made for building renovation or internal reconstruction, and so lines PP and VV cross at year Q. After this the site value will exceed that of the property value and a rational owner would find it preferable either to renovate the property, or to demolish and construct a new one, since to leave it as it is will mean the loss of additional profits. Where renovation has taken place then the line PP will be offset to the right, and the date at which the rational owner should decide to rebuild will be correspondingly moved farther into the future.

Figure 1 Economic life of a property

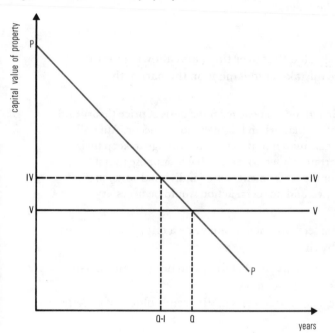

Figure 2 Changes in the economic life of a property

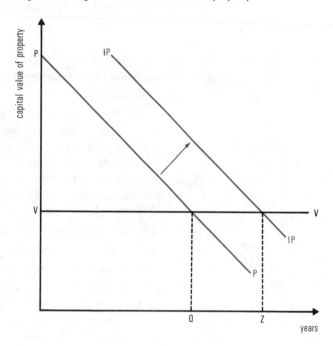

If site values were to increase rather than remain static as shown in line IV/IV then the time of decision will come not in year Q but in year Q-I. Such changes could take place where continued city growth results in greater space demands in central areas, or from the operation of planners in controlling building heights and densities elsewhere within the city. They could also result from the construction of new lines of communication creating new development modes.

However, such changes could also result in an increasing demand for building space of the type provided within the property itself and thus the line PP could be extended outwards from its original position to a new position IP/IP and the redevelopment point could be changed to Z (Figure 2).

Continuous changes in the site and property values as shown in Figures 1 and 2 could mean either that redevelopment will be modified markedly from the original point Q, and under some circumstances this point may never be reached.

In the real world, however, the site owner must take into account the costs of demolishing the property already on the site. He also needs to consider the capital value of the new building when constructed, and of course the costs of constructing it in the first place. After making an allowance for the maintenance costs of the new building, Goodall (1972) has suggested the following equations:

$$S_N = Y_N - C_N - O_N - D_E$$

where S_N is the site value in the new use, Y_N the present capital value of the expected earnings of the use of the new building, C_N the costs of constructing the new building, O_N the maintenance and operating costs of the new building, and D_E the costs of demolishing the existing building. As long as the existing value of the site and property exceeds that of the new value the existing building should be retained. Similarly if

$$Y_N \geq C_N + O_N + B_E$$

then redevelopment is not worthwhile where B_E equals present value of the existing building: whereas if

$$Y_N \leq C_N + O_N + D_E + B_E$$

then redevelopment should take place.

2 Why not the most profitable land use?

From the above it might be expected that over time, and allowing for the diffusion of information or the mistaken judgement on the part of the owner or developer:

> ... It might seem plausible at first glance to believe on the basis of price theory and the profit maximization assumption that urban blight could not occur. After all, would not profit-maximizing individuals find it to their advantage to keep their property in a state of repair? Certainly it seems reasonable to suppose that if individual benefits from repair or redevelopment exceed individual costs, then individual action could be expected and no social action would be necessary. (Whinston and Davis 1961)

That this does not occur can be seen whenever one visits a city. The next part of this unit is an analysis of why this is so.

One approach towards explaining why market forces do not present urban blight is to list some imperfections of the market:

1 There may not be a single owner but a series of different holders of *property rights* over the land.
2 The owner or holders of the property rights may not be aware of changes in site values, or may not be fully aware of their property values or costs, especially in times of rapid change.
3 He or they may not have the capital to change the site use by demolition and construction. He or they may have no wish to do so, or alternatively may not have a long enough lease to make a change of use profitable. Obviously if there is only five years of a lease left then redevelopment costs could probably not be repaid before the leasehold reverted to the freeholder.
4 The lease may contain a *restrictive covenant* preventing a change of use.
5 The site may not be large enough, by itself, to allow efficient redevelopment.
6 He or they may have both the interest and capital to redevelop his property but may not be able to without planning permission. This is true where the new property would involve a different land use, for example the demolition of housing to make way for offices. If it is held that this development would be detrimental to the city then development would not be possible.
7 Finally the owner of certain types of property, notably residential sitting tenants, may be unable to sell or redevelop the site because of statutory control, for example rent control.

An alternative way is to itemize the reasons why, within the housing market, not all groups utilize their resources in such a way as to realize its most efficient site use, ie why some owners are not optimizers. Some reasons have been well described by Cullingworth in *Housing in Transition*, a study of landlords and landowners in Lancaster. Following suggestions by Cullingworth one could group owners into:

1 Those who are concerned with gaining a living from property ownership without major effort or further investment.
2 Those who regard land-ownership as an adjunct to the use of the property for their own residential purposes.
3 Those who regard their property as a home, and a repository of memories of their past life, or as an investment for their future life.

In addition, other groups who own, or use, property without direct economic optimization as their goal, are:

4 Those who use the property as a base for a business and who are not prepared to capitalize on their site value for direct profit maximization. For example, a run-down property with low overheads and convenient links to others has certain advantages to the small business, and the internal advantages of not redeveloping and moving may exceed any economic argument stressing the need to do this.
5 Those who regard land in some symbolic way. The ownership of land provides a certain social background to a person and its retention simply as a symbol of success or social class may be of considerable importance.
6 Those who regard the ownership of property as a way of providing for a social need, eg municipal housing or property owned by philanthropic trusts, such as the Peabody Estate.

It might therefore appear that the property owner is very much constrained by his investment and attitudes and it is surprising not that so little spontaneous redevelopment takes place but that so much does. Certainly such factors can provide an insight into why urban areas tend to become potentially less economically efficient as time passes. The underlying problem is that buildings once constructed are fixed with much capital tied up in their infrastructure. They cannot change their uses suddenly in response to the market changes. The lot of the property owner is, however, eased over time, since after a period, the capital in any building has been repaid from its profits and future profitability of the site will then depend simply on the difference between incomings from rents and leases and outgoings to rates and maintenance.

3 The patterns of change

We have now looked at the generalized economic factors that affect property and site values within the city once initial development has been completed. We have also looked at the different motives of holders of property rights. Their actions will depend upon the interactions between these motives. However before discussing changes in detail it is of advantage to look at the spatial extent of residential areas within the city, especially in relation to the age of development.

The pattern of the city within the developed world reflects a steady population growth. This is true in relation to both Europe and North America, and it can be illustrated by reference to any city that you know well.

For example if we look at Norwich (see Figure 3) we can see how development spread outwards in all directions from the central core of the Cathedral and Castle. The map shows a series of rough collars of development from the early

Plate 1 Typical high density inner city housing constructed during the 1860s

eighteenth century to the present day. There is a general trend from older properties near the city centre to newer ones on the periphery, though older types may occur peripherally if other settlements have been incorporated into a larger city. This trend has been described and commented upon for a considerable period of time (see discussions in the D100 and D281 courses). Kirwan and Martin (1972) in their study of residential improvement drew upon a random sample of families to interview (see Table 1), and found the following:

Table 1 Age of owner-occupied housing by area and distance from town centre, North East Lancashire

	Distance from town centre									
	Up to 0.9 kms		1.0–1.9 kms		2.0–2.9 kms		3.0 kms and over		Total	
	No	%	No	%	No	%	No	%	No	%
Accrington										
Pre-1880	27	54.0	3	14.3					30	40.0
1881–1914	15	30.0	12	57.1	2	50.0			29	38.7
1915–1944	5	10.0	3	14.3					8	10.6
1945 onwards	3	6.0	3	14.3	2	50.0			8	10.6
Total	50	100.0	21	100.0	4	100.0			75	100.0
Blackburn										
Pre-1880	17	70.8	26	24.3	4	9.1	3	21.4	50	26.5
1881–1914	7	29.2	66	61.7	23	52.3	3	21.4	99	52.4
1915–1944			10	9.3	11	25.0	6	42.8	27	14.3
1945 onwards			5	4.7	6	13.6	2	14.4	13	6.8
Total	24	100.0	107	100.0	44	100.0	14	100.0	189	100.0
Burnley										
Pre-1880	7	43.8	12	13.5					19	13.9
1881–1914	9	56.2	61	68.5	8	29.6			78	56.9
1915–1944			8	9.0	14	51.9	3	60.0	25	18.2
1945 onwards			8	9.0	5	18.5	2	40.0	15	11.0
Total	16	100.0	89	100.0	27	100.0	5	100.0	137	100.0
Nelson										
Pre-1880	28	44.4							28	33.7
1881–1914	33	52.4	13	65.0					46	55.4
1915–1944	2	3.2	7	35.0					9	10.9
1945 onwards										
Total	63	100.0	20	100.0					83	100.0

Source: Kirwan and Martin (1972)

Figure 3 Peripheral development over time Source: City Planning Office, Norwich

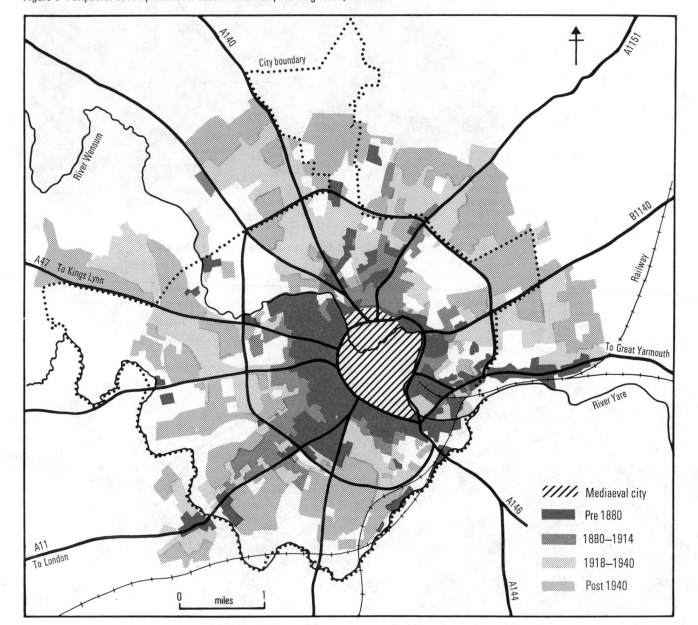

Therefore the oldest properties tend to be situated on the more valuable city centre sites. Over time, as the city grows peripherally, these sites become relatively more central. Increasing centrality means that they are increasingly accessible and this in turn leads to rising site values. One must contrast this with the way in which the buildings themselves are becoming older and tending to weaken structurally. At the same time they will be becoming less attuned to the needs and aspirations of users, which as they reflect general societal goals, change continuously.

Consider, for example, an area of residential property constructed near any major centre during the 1880s, eg Norwich (Figure 3). This area would have been constructed peripherally to the city (using the cheapest land available at the time). It would probably be some two to three miles from the centre, and would thus be within walking distance. It would have been constructed to suit the potential market. If this market was the artisan, then bearing in mind the low disposable incomes of this group in the nineteenth century, the housing would have needed to be relatively inexpensive. Densities would have

Plate 2 Over time areas may become progressively more in need of attention

been high, gardens probably absent (though back yards might have been present), internal services would have consisted of individual coal fires in each room, perhaps gas for cooking and lighting, and possibly a cold water tap (although not essential). If the market had been the middle class then space

Figure 4 A typical inner city housing layout Source: City Planning Office, Norwich

☐ General improvement area
◻ Roads
Scale 1:1250

standards would have been far higher within the house itself (including space for servants), but the physical infrastructure would have been much the same.

Between this period and the present day demands have changed and statutory controls introduced through Building Regulations and By-Laws. Some of these are:

1 Space demands per person have increased.
2 Controls on adults of different sexes sleeping in the same rooms have been introduced.
3 Damp courses are now mandatory.
4 Heat insulation is demanded.
5 Central heating is replacing the individual fire.
6 Hot water is expected within the house.
7 Individual bathrooms and separate kitchens are expected.
8 Car parking space is expected.
9 Noise insulation is expected and is a marketable commodity.
10 Individual plot size is often expected to be larger.

Whilst these demands and controls apply only fully to new houses, it is only to be expected that the house purchaser will measure the desirability of older property in these terms. So whilst some of these improvements will no doubt have been incorporated in some properties, in many others they cannot easily be put into effect. Thus the desirability of this property in relation to the new will have fallen, and this will be reflected in its market value.

4 The property owner

The problems facing the property owner in the inner city may be summarized as:

1 An increasing space need for living, or, in the case of commercial property, for putting in machines or equipment.
2 An increasing demand for complex services.
3 An increasing need for external facilities, such as car parking.
4 An increasing rate burden. Since rates are assessed upon a nominal letting valuation then a more accessible location will be rated at a high value if the property is nearer the city centre than if it is farther away.
5 The need continuously to keep the physical structure of the property in a safe condition. This last problem affects all owners, of course, but will tend to be most acute in older properties.

So the owner is placed in a position where he needs to take into account his increasing site value, and at the same time the problems that face him. In the idealized economic structure suggested earlier he has certain options open to him. If his own goals make him a financial or an economic optimizer then he can renovate and improve, or demolish and reconstruct. If he has other motives for holding the property rights his choice may differ. In practice his freedom to choose between options will be limited by financial, legal or planning constraints.

4.1 Constraints upon private renewal: financial

To make any change in the *status quo*, and to realize either on the increased site value, or on a potential increase in the property value will involve a capital expenditure. Even to maintain the *status quo* if the external environment is changing may involve expenditure. For example, if traffic noise is becoming an increasing nuisance then unless the owner wants his property value to decline he must find ways of excluding noise from the property. This might well be expensive if double glazing insulation or air conditioning are considered. Rewiring a building to take into account the increasing use of domestic electric appliances may cost in excess of £500 for even a small building.

An indication of the expenditure incurred in merely maintaining property in a reasonable condition can be seen when one looks at the data in Table 2.

Table 2 Total expenditure on repairs and improvements per dwelling, North East Lancashire, 1965–70

	%
£0–199	58.8
£200–399	23.2
£400–599	15.5
£600 and over	2.5
Total	100.0

Source: Kirwan and Martin (1972)

It will be necessary to find this money somewhere, and unless the owner has sufficient reserves he must borrow it. This needs some security, and may not be easy to produce. One major problem here is that most older central properties are on small plots. The potential site value depends not only on plot size but on potential use if joined to other plots to make a site of developable size. So whereas site values might exceed £100,000 an acre in inner London, an owner who owns say one-tenth of an acre has not a site of £10,000 value. This plot by itself could not be used for a land use capable of paying the full sum per acre.

If the owner is concerned with a flow of receipts from the property (for example rents), then any improvement must be paid for by increased rents. The owner must therefore be able to show that he will receive these before he can obtain financial backing. This introduces the concept of legal constraints.

4.2 Legal constraints   The whole question of the law of property is extremely complex, and its common law base has been much modified by legislation and precedent. Even to summarize fully the main points relevant to urban renewal would prove to be time consuming for you. However, some main points will be of value in your understanding of urban change.

Firstly, all land has a *freehold owner*. The basic situation has been summarized by James (1962):

... The ordinary purchaser of land probably pictures himself as acquiring a certain visible portion of the earth's surface. In fact the law entitles him to something more than this, for, broadly speaking, in the eye of the law, 'land' includes the surface of the land, everything beneath the surface, and everything affixed to the land. Further, the right to land carries with it rights of property over things in the air-space above the land. (James 1962)

Over time, however, two things have happened. Firstly, various rights over land have been removed. For example, aircraft do not need the permission of all freeholders to overfly land, neither does the owner have a free right to exploit oil, coal or natural gas found on his land. Secondly, many freeholders have sold *leases* on their property, and these *leaseholders* may have sold shorter leases to others.

In a lease the freeholder gives away certain rights, eg the right to erect property for a certain number of years. Any time period may be specified although conventionally it is 999 or 99 years. In exchange he receives a down payment, an annual payment, or both. At the end of the agreed period the land, rights, and any property on it reverts to the freeholder. To prevent irreparable harm to his property the freeholder may insist that the leaseholder does not do certain things, eg run a business. Such controls are termed *restrictive covenants*.

Society has felt in the past that leasehold reversion (ie the lease returning to the freeholder) can lead to inequity, and various statutes exist limiting the rights of the freeholder in this matter, though in general terms they still exist.

If the owner of a site and property in the city is a freeholder then he has few legal constraints upon his actions. If he is a leaseholder then in addition to any problems resulting from restrictive covenants, the length that the lease, or agreement, has to run will be important. If it is a long time it might be worth his while to redevelop as he can recoup his costs in the time still available. However, he might be under a restrictive covenant that prevents certain actions, so his freedom might be somewhat limited. If little time is left before the lease expires it is not worthwhile incurring capital costs since the property plus any improvements will revert to the freeholder before the leaseholder can gain from them.

As suggested earlier, a ninety-nine year lease is common. You can thus see that development that took place during the 1850s and 1860s was coming to the end of its lease during the 1950s and 1960s, and reconstruction or improvement were less attractive than they otherwise might have been at this time.

However, some leaseholders and tenants have the right to extend their leases, and in some cases to pay rents or ground rent (the annual payment of a leaseholder to a freeholder) reflecting what they had always paid, not the current rate. This means that the freedom of the freeholder to renovate for a new leaseholder, or to gain possession for redevelopment has been very much limited. The exact wording of past and present agreements is of vital importance here, and the whole process is one involving considerable legal dexterity on both sides.

Even if the owner has the ability under law to reconstruct, his unconditional right to do so has been lost under the 1947 Town and Country Act continued in the 1962 and 1968 Acts. He must obtain planning permission to carry out major modifications, demolish and reconstruct, or change the use of his property.

4.3 Planning constraints

Under the 1968 Town and Country Planning Act all development must, in general terms, obtain planning permission before it can go ahead. The owner or user of a property or its site must apply to the Local Planning Authority to get this. Permission can be refused, granted unconditionally, or with conditions. The planning process is thus one of considerable importance in the land and property market. By granting or withholding permissions in large numbers the planner can increase or decrease the market value of different properties. The word *planner* above is somewhat of a misnomer, however. To understand what is meant here it is probably worth conceptualizing the planning process in Britain (see Figure 5).

From this it can be seen that the planner acts only on instructions from the politician (elected representative). He is the decision maker, the professional planner must content himself with providing information and implementing previously agreed policies. In land use planning, therefore, explicit or implicit policies adopted by the Local Planning Authority will, in time, create a conformity between actual and policy derived land users. This means that if the planner decides from his analysis that an area contains enough of a particular land use and if his advice is accepted, then no further development of this type will be allowed. This will in turn limit the possible site values in the area.

In practice, of course, this limit is not absolute both because of any general increase of land values, and because of speculation. But the fact that a particular

Figure 5 A conceptualized model of the planning process

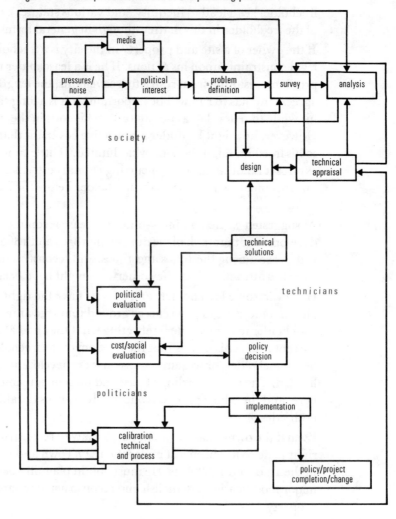

type of development is not acceptable now does not mean that *this will be always so*. Sites may therefore be of interest as long term investments, or simply because it is felt that there might be a change in the short term.

In areas within which development of a particular nature is permitted then values are likely to rise at a rate faster than normal. This reflects any unsatisfied demand to the refusal of planning permissions in other areas.

If we refer back to Figure 5 we can see that within the planning process there is a stage when alternative schemes are being evaluated in economic or social terms. After this stage whether or not they progress to action will depend upon political considerations, legal feasibility and on capital availability (or even whether they need to be phased in with other policies), and their existence will be public knowledge.

Suppose, for example, there is a proposal for a new inner area road. Its line is planned to run through a residential area, and it is to be built when finance is available. An owner on the route cannot reasonably redevelop or modify his property with any certainty of having time to recoup his investment. If permission to do so is applied for it is unlikely to be granted, since it might prejudice the scheme should finance be forthcoming. The market value of the property even in its existing condition will be affected. New owners are unlikely to purchase without a guarantee that they can make use of it for some time into the future.

Until 1972 it was difficult to obtain compensation. Now, however, it is proposed that owner occupiers can claim compensation if affected by road schemes. All other proposals, however, carry no right to compensation unless the owner can prove that this threat prevents any economic use of land at all – a very difficult thing to prove. In such cases properties are usually termed *blighted*, and the whole process has been referred to as *planning blight*. It is a problem facing all property owners or users in a society that accepts compulsory purchase as a necessity.

4.4 Summary

The site and property owner finds that over time his freedom of action to make use of changes of the value of his property is affected by financial, legal and planning restraints. The situation is well summed up by Rothenberg:

... Slum homeowners are likely to have low incomes. But depreciation on their old dwellings makes necessary substantial maintenance expenses, sometimes major repairs. Their own resources are likely to be too meager, and their efforts to borrow from private sources are almost invariably frustrated. Loans through conventional channels are very nearly unobtainable. When they can be obtained, interest rates are likely to be quite high, thus cutting down the demand. The credit available for housing in these areas is typically undercover financing at very high interest rates for dealers in speculative housing. This encourages not maintenance but conversion of dwellings to slum use.

Second, the situation is somewhat the same for landlords. Low-income rentals often involve tenants who have only slight stakes in the community, often recently migrated from rural, culturally different societies, with little appreciation of the necessary disciplines involved in urban living. Their occupancy is very likely to accelerate markedly the depreciation of their dwelling units. Again adequate maintenance is likely to be very expensive, and, when major repairs are needed, it is likely to be thwarted by the unavailability of credit. Thus, the rapid, even accelerated, depreciation of property makes upkeep onerous. This is enough to induce some homeowners to skimp on maintenance and to risk code violations. For landlords it provides a temptation to skimp; but this temptation is not enough to provoke violation, if to do so would mean weakening their market position *vis-à-vis* tenants. But tenants in these poor areas are likely to have very low bargaining power in the market. They have little wealth, little mobility, highly inadequate knowledge of alternatives, and – as is disproportionately true in slums – they are discriminated against in housing as in employment, education and political influence. (Rothenberg in Stewart 1972 pp 140–1)

Rothenberg here summarizes the different problems facing different groups of land users. So far in this unit we have tended to consider those with an interest in land and property as a homogenous group, though we have discussed the different reasons for owning land and property. However, when it comes to looking at ways in which land users react to economic pressures it is worthwhile accepting the Rothenberg definitions of different groups.

Firstly we have owner occupiers. These may be freeholders or leaseholders, but they use the property themselves, either for residence or business purposes. They are concerned more with its use therefore, than for its potential as a capital asset. Secondly there are landlords. They may also be freeholders or leaseholders, but they own the property in order to profit from it. This they may do either in the form of receipts from rents, or by selling it and realizing its capital value. Thirdly there are the tenants, who pay rents, and are thus wholly concerned with its use rather than value.

We might now ask ourselves what is the owner of land and property within the inner city going to do. He is hemmed in by legal, financial and planning restrictions, and is therefore in a declining competitive position. In many cases, especially if an owner occupier, he may do nothing at all. This is true if he is satisfied with his existing property use. He may sell out and move elsewhere, and thereby gain from any increased site value, but in view of the constraints already described this may be difficult to obtain.

If he is a landlord he may take alternative courses of action. He could amalgamate his holdings if they are spatially contiguous so that he could redevelop the site in a more profitable way. Or he could try to find users willing to pay higher rents.

Changes in tastes and aspirations may have rendered the property unsuitable for the original market. Other markets (persons) may find it increasingly attractive, for example families with different aspirations or with lower incomes and an inability to satisfy their aspirations, may do so (especially if coupled with good accessibility). If the household cannot afford to pay for much space per person then the owner can increase his residential densities within the older property. Subdivision can take place. Subdivision will include a cost to the owner (the provision of separate as well as communal facilities), but this additional cost can be recouped in a short time by increased receipts from multiple occupation. Return on capital and on the site value is increased. This leads to the apparently anomalous position in most European or North American orientated cities where low income families live within areas of high land or site values. However, each individual family or household controls only a small area of land. Profits for the site as a whole arise from combining profits from each separate unit and total profits from multiple occupation will reflect the high land values.

In summary the operation of the land market within urban areas is such as to create a narrowing gap between site and property values unless the owner has the resources, ability and willingness continuously to redevelop, modernize or increase the use intensity of his land.

5 The social background

So far we have concentrated on the problems of change in relation to those economic forces that have a direct bearing on the property or site owner. In many cases, however, the site landlord does not physically live in the area, and at most his occupation may be limited to a few hours a day. It is therefore now necessary to look at the social problems created by those economic forces acting on those living within inner city residential areas. Some of these problems are described elsewhere within the course, notably in Unit 9, 'Social Segregation of the Slum'.

The general theme of social problems in areas suffering a decline has been summarized by Rothenberg as:

. . . Poor housing may easily be seen as an effective way to economize desperately scarce purchasing power. Moreover, it may be the easiest sacrifice to make. Hunger and cold are immediate pains and are barriers to holding gainful employment in a way that dirty, old overcrowded living quarters are not. (Rothenberg in Stewart 1972 p 134)

Now let us look at how these problems are created, noting that the above quotation, even though it is discussing a social problem, is framed in economic terms.

The absence of capital for improvement tends to lead to an increase in the density of use in residential property. This means that living space per household will be low and that internal services will tend to be poor or even absent.

Where provided they will often be overused, leading to unreliability. Lease and tenancies will tend to be on very short terms (reflecting the operation of leasehold and other tenure laws) creating considerable tenure insecurity. Externally the environment will be degraded. Such overuse of some facilities and the absence of others can lead to problems of human stress. McHarg (1969) has shown how physical disease, eg tuberculosis, diabetes, syphilis, bacillary dysentery, and salmonellosis, social disease such as homicide, rape, alcholism, and drug addiction, rise with increasing living densities. Leyhausen (1965) has documented problems of mental health arising from such conditions of stress. Further, the absence of community facilities, again reflecting the original design characteristics of the areas, tends to lead to increased road accident risk (children forced to play in streets) and towards family breakdown.

Why then do people choose to live in such areas? Firstly, in order to move into a more secure tenure some capital is required, either in the form of a down-payment or because mortgages and loans require some type of security. Many families are unable to meet this requirement. Secondly, families may be transient and may not wish for security of tenure since this is accompanied by an obligation to reside for some period of time. Thirdly, family income may fluctuate, especially if employment is insecure, and any commitment to anything but the lower costs for the shortest time cannot be borne. Fourthly, such families may not meet the requirements for municipal or council property. There is usually a residence qualification, and until residence over time is confirmed a move is not possible. In most cases the construction of municipal housing has not matched demand and results in a waiting list.

Fifthly, housing costs are only one part of the household budget. As Alonso (1964) defined it, 'an individual's income equals the amount spent on land costs + commuting costs + all other expenditure'. If disposable incomes are fixed in a family, then an increase in land (property) costs to the household must be met by a reduction in travel or other expenditure. If it is impossible to reduce expenditure on food, clothes, etc, then to move farther from the workplace (meaning increased commuting costs) without a reduction in property costs, is not possible. In some cases families in such a position cannot move out, even if peripheral municipal property with lower rents is available.

It has already been suggested that once a property has been constructed its users have gradually changed in character. Households move in great numbers each year (up to twenty per cent per annum in the UK). As opportunities and aspirations change, those with the ability to meet these migrate towards more satisfactory property. People *filter* from small towards larger property, from one suburban zone to another being constructed further from the city centre, and so on. In the past they have been replaced by others moving towards their own aspiration levels. Such a spiral action can operate both upwards and downwards. This leads towards an unstable situation with a transient population. Stability will be reached only when groups with similar aspirations locate in the same area and are unwilling or unable to move again. This can occur at any level, and such stability encourages interaction. It may lead to group norms or ideals, or even to grouped family structures through intermarriage, and the development of subcultures. Community identification, if only identification in the face of physical and environmental conditions, acts as the basis of much of the quality of life in such areas. It appears that it may be this cohesiveness that allows long term residence in declining areas, and keeps physical, mental and social disorders at lower levels in certain parts of inner city areas than in others.

The stability maintained in this way may, however, have inherent problems within it if the stable group are economically able to follow their aspirations but are prevented from doing so by other groups. As suggested earlier, property within the inner city can provide cheap housing and may provide a social group with a similar cultural background for the newly arrived urban dweller, whether a migrant from rural areas or from overseas. A proportion of these dwellers will, over time, become economically stable enough to move out into better housing and environmental conditions. To move out they must, however, find somewhere to go, and if they are part of a group that is not welcomed elsewhere this may act to turn them back into the area.

In the United States this is the problem facing the negro. Morrill (1965) describes the problem as:

... The impact of the ghetto on the life of its residents is partly well known, partly hidden. The white person driving through is struck by the poverty, the substandard housing, the mixture of uses, and the dirt; he is likely to feel that these conditions are due to the innate character of the Negro. The underlying fact is, of course, that Negroes on the average are much poorer, owing partly to far inferior educational opportunities in most areas, but more to systematic discrimination in employment, which is only now beginning to be broken. Besides pure poverty, pressure of the influx into most northern cities itself induces deterioration: formerly elegant houses, abandoned by whites, have had to be divided and redivided to accommodate the newcomers, maintenance is almost impossible, much ownership is by absentee whites. Public services, such as street maintenance and garbage collection, and amenities, such as parks and playgrounds, are often neglected. Residential segregation means *de facto* school segregation. Unemployment is high, at least double the white average, and delinquency and crime are the almost inevitable result. A feeling of inferiority and hopelessness comes to pervade the ghetto. Most important is the enormous waste of human resources in the failure to utilize Negroes to reasonable capacity. The real cost of maintaining the ghetto system is fantastic. In direct costs the city spends much more in crime prevention, welfare payments, and so forth than it can collect. The ghetto is the key to the Negro problem.

What are the forces that operate to maintain the ghetto system? Four kinds of barriers hinder change: prejudice of whites against Negroes; characteristics of the Negroes; discrimination by the real-estate industry and associated financial institutions; and legal and governmental barriers. Naked prejudice is disclaimed by a majority of Americans today. Today's prejudice is not an outright dislike; it is, rather, a subtle fear, consisting of many elements. The typical white American may now welcome the chance to meet a Negro, but he is afraid that if a Negro moves into his neighbourhood it will break up and soon be all Negro. Of course, on a national average there are not as many Negroes as that – only one or two families to a block – but the fear exists because that is the way the ghetto has grown. A greater fear is of loss in social status if Negroes move in. This reflects the culture-bred notion that Negroes are inherently of lower standing. Some persons are terrified at the unlikely prospect of intermarriage. Finally, people are basically afraid of, or uncertain about, people who are different, especially in any obvious physical way. These fears combine into powerful controls to maintain segregation: refusal to sell to Negroes, so as not to offend the neighbors; and the tendency to move out as soon as a Negro enters, in order not to lose status by association. (Morrill 1965)

From this it may appear that the problem is tied only to colour prejudice. It is partly, but the process is not new. In the past, New York has experienced the same thing in relation to Poles, Ukrainians, Puerto Ricans and Irish to name but four nationalities. Most cities have traditionally had Jewish quarters, reflecting historically the same type of pressures.

Over time such social diffusion and filtering both in and out of areas has created marked internal social divisions within areas of similar property type and age, and created areas of transience, stability, tension and stress within the inner city. Overall the inner city provides a service through the availability of low cost and highly accessible property. Such areas can be regarded as being the products of the absence of capital, ie poverty, but at the same time they ameliorate some of the hardships of poverty.

Inner city areas showing the features described above can be found in any part of the world where urban development has a long history and where city growth has been continuous. To gain an insight into the scale you can look at surveys of the age of buildings within England and Wales. Of course many properties are not within city areas, but since eighty per cent of the population lives within urban areas it is to be expected that the largest proportion of housing is within a city of some sort.

It was estimated in 1967 that some 6,459,000 dwellings in use in England and Wales dated from before 1918. This was forty-six per cent of the total housing stock (Table 3).

Table 3 Estimates of houses by date of construction, England and Wales

Dates of construction	1961*		1967†	
	No (000s)	%	No (000s)	%
Before 1880	3,666	25.6 }	6,459	46.0
1881–1918	3,000	20.9		
1919–1944	4,333	30.2	4,255	30.4
1945–date of survey	3,333	23.3	3,300	23.6
Total	14,332	100.0	14,014	100.0

Sources: *Housing in England and Wales, Cmnd 1290, HMSO, 1961
†Old houses into new homes, Cmnd 3602, HMSO, 1968

From Table 4 you can see that 77.7 per cent of all rented property was constructed prior to 1919.

Table 4 Age of houses by tenure 1960, England and Wales (in 000s)

	Private Rented	%	Owner Occupied	%	Local Authority	%	All Types	%
Pre 1919	3,258	77.7	2,707	45.1	245	7.1	6,210	45.6
1919–1944	730	17.4	2,357	39.3	1,157	33.7	6,244	31.1
1945–1960	203	4.9	934	15.6	2,033	59.2	3,170	23.3
Total	4,191	100.0	5,998	100.0	3,435	100.0	15,624	100.0

Source: Gray and Russell (1962)

Certain cities have more than a proportional share of older properties and of properties in need of repair or renovation. For example, Cullingworth and Watson (1972) found that for Glasgow forty-two per cent of all properties was deficient in services or in need of structural improvement.

Table 5 Housing condition in Clydeside, 1970

Housing condition	Owns/buying %	Public authority %	Rents/Private unfurnished %	Other %	Total %
Good	48	75	16	44	56
Fair	5	—	6	—	2
One or more structural defect	33	23	46	24	30
No inside WC	14	2	32	32	12
Sample base	300	738	296	50	1,484

Source: Housing in Clydeside, 1970, HMSO, 1971, p 60

In addition, only twenty-two per cent of rented property was in good or fair condition. It is also interesting to note that twenty-five per cent of municipally owned property was in a similar state but this reflects in part the purchase by the city of property prior to demolition. To get an indication of the total number of properties in Glasgow that were below a tolerable standard of accommodation we can refer to Dennis (1972), in which he quotes the estimate by the City Council that some 75,000 individual properties were substandard and in need of some governmental or municipal action, out of a total of 310,000 properties.

To show that this is not an isolated case one can look at Liverpool in 1972 and see the extent of areas in need of improvement (Figure 6).

Figure 6 Urban renewal and urban reception areas of Liverpool Source: Stones (1972)

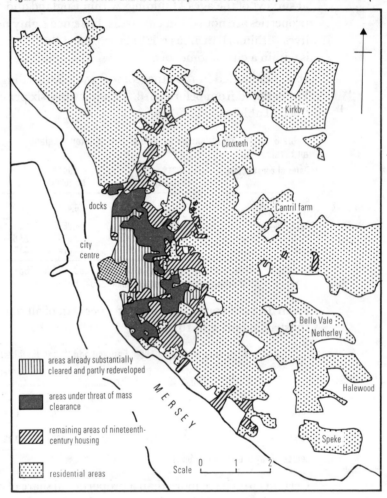

Properties and areas reaching the end of their useful life, will be found within any urban area. Their exact location will differ from city to city depending upon the development characteristics of the city from 50 to 200 years ago. For example, inner city areas within Manchester in such a state in the early 1960s were Ardwick, Hulme, Moss Side and Cheetham Hill. These, plus other areas, formed a collar ringing the city centre at a distance of between a half and three miles from the centre. During the past decade many of these areas have been redeveloped but new areas have now reached the same state, for example Rusholme. This process has been well described by Keyes (1969) for Boston with its blighted areas of Charlestown, South End and Washington Park.

The criteria used to define properties or areas reaching the end of their useful life will of course determine their spatial description. If all properties in excess of fifty years were included then obsolete housing would account for perhaps forty per cent of urban property. However, not all such properties are in reality becoming blighted. Renovation may have taken place. Continuous upkeep may have been maintained. Planning blight may not exist. The properties may have been constructed with a longer economic life and with services and facilities closer to modern needs than the norm. Alternatively, if 'slum' properties only were described, then the extent of such areas would be far more limited in scale and more spatially discontinuous.

On introducing the word 'slum', however, a value judgement has been made. From a technical planning viewpoint a slum is a property unfit for human habitation or use. As you will see later, in the United Kingdom this definition is extremely important in relation to urban renewal since it defines a whole range of compensatory procedures and is an important factor in determining the type of renewal that is possible. The interpretation of the definition is made by the local public health inspector using guidelines relating among other things to rising damp, vermin, structural conditions and the absence of facilities. These are all internal to the property. External factors such as the general environmental standard of the area are not included. It was estimated in 1960 that in England and Wales there were 622,000 property units already in this state; that there were 210,000 units that would reach this state within five years (from 1960) and that as a total some 1,954,000 properties would be in such a state by 1975 (Gray and Russell 1962).

This is a very large number and over the past decades municipal interest in areas showing deterioration has increased. From this interest has come curative or palliative action. Such action has depended upon:
1 a definition of areas as problem areas;
2 the goals and objectives against which to measure problem and solutions.

The recognition of slum areas as problems is not new. For example in 1875 the Artizans and Labourers Dwelling and Improvement Act was passed in England. This recognized the effects of poor living conditions and set minimum housing standards. Parliament saw the problem as one with a direct cause and effect. Poor housing standards (overcrowding, absence of facilities, dampness and so forth) were regarded as causing disease, family breakup, a dislike of honest work and a tendency to commit crime. It was argued that if basic housing conditions could be changed then the resultant problems would cease.

A similar somewhat moralistic note is struck by the definition of a slum in the 1937 Housing Act of the United States:

. . . 'Slum' means any area where dwellings predominate which, by reason of dilapidation, overcrowding, faulty arrangements of design, lack of ventilation, light or sanitation facilities, or any combination of these factors are detrimental to *safety, health or morals*.

Such an approach has, both in the United States and the United Kingdom, resulted in a definition of urban problems in terms of the physical environment.

Unfortunately, not all aspects of the situation within the inner city fit such a problem definition. Poor living conditions will not only have direct effects upon users and inhabitants, but will create environmental hazards to whole areas, and can result in a deterioration of the 'quality of life'. Structurally, buildings might be sound. They could, however, be adversely effected by external factors, for example traffic noise. The absence of external facilities, such as parks or public open space, may further lower this quality.

Secondly, social problems may arise only indirectly from the physical state of the properties in an area. As people with the ability to meet their aspirations move out, they will tend to be replaced with those of lower economic abilities and aspirations. These newcomers plus the original residents forced to remain behind by economic necessity will be less able to pay for services than their predecessors. Rates are used to provide the basis of municipal finance in most of the western world. These only marginally reflect any increase in the intensity of property use. The result tends to be an increasing burden on those who can pay (encouraging further out-migration), on the commercial and industrial properties (reducing their profitability), or on those who can least afford to pay in the form of increased rates, ie the migrants. This leads, in turn, to an urban financing problem. It is one facing most cities. Even allowing for central government aid it is of general concern to any city authority.

Also resulting from the trend of the migration of families with higher skills and aspirations away from disadvantaged areas is a problem of local democratic leadership. Since local government depends on democratic control, some form of democratic elite with the education and ability fully to represent people and control policies is needed. Yet it is this type of person who is absent. A gap will then develop between the municipal authority and its population. Severe communication problems may well be created.

6 Urban renewal policies

There is no single solution to the problems facing the inner city. At different times and in different cities many alternatives have been tried and different attempts have been made to control the problem from the national down to the street corner level.

... It would be more accurate to call any given city's urban-renewal activity a collection of projects rather than a programme. Projects have been initiated as the result of local pressure to get rid of the worst blight first, to satisfy special interest groups, to clear areas with great market potential, or to combine renewal with other capital improvement programmes. In very few cases has there been any effort to tie the projects to a city-wide strategy. (Wallace 1968)

Such a criticism is perhaps somewhat harsh since the actions that can be taken, and thus the overall strategy that can be adopted, depend upon a series of interrelated factors, and these vary not only at the inter-city but also intra-city level. They can be described as social-economic forces, legal constraints, financial resources, and the perception of the situation. As you will have noted they are directly comparable with those facing the private owner of inner-city property. The one difference being that the municipal authority is in a position generally to plan its own development, ie is much less affected by planning control than the private owner, since it is its own planning authority.

It is also most important to remember the urban change and renewal process is one that is continuously taking place anyway. It is not always termed a problem, and even if it is, it is only one of many facing a government. It must not be thought of in isolation. Other policies, such as the improvement of CBD access, will have implications that will affect both the problem and possible solutions.

In general terms the possible solutions to the problem of the decay of the inner city are threefold:

1 To allow spontaneous redevelopment by interested individuals.

2 To modify the social or economic forces operating in such areas so that redevelopment becomes acceptable and profitable for individual owners.

3 To redevelop compulsorily and reconstruct the property within these areas.

6.1 Spontaneous redevelopment

It has been suggested earlier that the economic forces operating within the inner city may lead to either property or environmental degradation, and often to both. This process is, however, not irreversible even in a relatively unconstrained economic system. If demand for land increases faster than a supply is made available then site values will increase rapidly enough to make the demolition of property and its renewal perfectly feasible. In this case, providing planning control is not onerous, the land can be redeveloped in a more efficient way. The developer (owner/landlord) will therefore either demolish and convert to a different and more economic land use, or will demolish and reconstruct with a more economic form of the same use. For residential areas this means either that residential property is being removed from the market, or that the nature of the residential property will change. If the developer is to get a better return from his capital, and at the same time capitalize on his increased site value, then he will need to attract tenants, or lessees able to pay higher rents. These will tend to differ from the original inhabitants, and the result will be that lower cost property is removed from the market. Alternatively, if demand for property is well above supply, then as values rise there can be an increase in rents and this will encourage structural improvements.

Around London, for example, external planning control is so restrictive that families wishing to move to suburban areas, find the 'Green Belt' and other policies have so reduced land supply that house prices rise rapidly and that the number of new house sites is falling. At the same time communication costs have been rising. The result has been a tendency for those with the aspirations and ability to move outwards, being forced to look inwards if they wish to purchase:

1 Properties with low communication costs.
2 Properties with much internal space per person.

This has meant families looking for older inner city property with more space per person than comparable new property, ie the older middle class house. Once purchased, improvements can be carried out secure in the knowledge that they will be repaid by increased property values. Over time such

Plate 3 A typical visual and environmental problem resulting from slum clearance

spontaneous renewal may well take place within parts of the inner city – but you should remember that it is a very selective process, and it only applies to existing residential property. It creates, however, its own problems. Firstly, the type of housing search is, as already suggested, selective. Properties chosen must be suitable for improvement, and will be fairly large. This will mean that properties already totally converted to multiple occupation are likely to remain so, either because of their high values (measured in return on capital) or because of the costs of reconversion into a single household unit. It will also mean that smaller, or more dilapidated properties are likely to stay the same. It is the larger house suitable for conversion that is sought.

There are several social implications of such a process. Firstly, there will be a reduction in the number of properties available to the existing population. Potential users will be priced out by potential improvers. Secondly, the possibility of conversion to multiple use will be reduced and this will mean a reduction in potential household spaces. Thirdly, property values in areas undergoing 'improvement' will rise. Over time this will be reflected in rises in rates charges, and an added cost will fall upon existing property owners.

In effect this causes an enforced emigration of the urban poor into an increasingly congested property market. So the situation facing these low income families is that rents will rise because of a decline in housing supply and a decline in their position in relation to the higher income groups being forced to look towards the inner city for accommodation. Social problems will be created both in areas involved and in others with similar characteristics.

This point is brought out by a report prepared by the Notting Hill Peoples Association Housing Group (1972). Referring to an area in North Kensington, London (Colville and Tavistock Neighbourhoods), they state 'The social and economic forces prevalent in these areas are creating a situation in which it is no longer possible for the resident low income people to live there.'

This statement is amplified by pointing out that in 1967 all the private rented accommodation in the area could be defined as low rent accommodation. The highest rents were £12.30 per week, the lowest £0.50 per week, with a mean rent of £4.50 per week. Since that date forty per cent of the property in the area has been converted. Of this forty per cent, twenty-four per cent has been emptied and relet at rents twice to five times higher than the 1967 figure,

Table 6 Rent increases 1967–72

Rents of unconverted and unadapted houses, 1967 and 1972		
	1967 All houses	1972 All unconverted & unadapted houses
Average	£4.50	£5.40
Highest	£12.30	£16.00
Lowest	£00.50	£1.30
Rent increases in 'converted'* houses		
	1967 rent	Rent after conversion (1972)
Average	£4.80	£14.50
Highest	£12.00	£25.00
Lowest	£1.00	£9.00
Rent increases in 'adapted' † houses		
	1967	1972
Average	£4.75	£9.50
Highest	£7.35	£19.00
Lowest	£2.15	£6.00

*Emptied, major alterations of condition and amenities, and improvement to a high standard

†Changed to bed-sit and small unit accommodation, either through landlords changing letting pattern or through conversion

and a further seven per cent is in the process of being relet. Of the remainder, nine per cent has been further subdivided and rents raised.

Even allowing for inflation it can be seen from Table 6 that rent increases have risen more than proportionately.

As a benefit, an articulate and more affluent group moving into an area may help regenerate local democracy. As a cost these people may implement sectarian interests that may discriminate against the original population.

Such a process may well tend to improve the physical environment of inner city areas. Houses will be improved and facilities less used. But it will not solve the human problems of the inner city. It will both make them worse and spread them. In practice it will convert areas of the private renting market back into areas of owner occupation, creating new demands on existing private rented property and also increasing demands upon municipal housing. The resultant costs will fall on both the local authority and the individual. Within the United Kingdom the loss of status amongst families moving to municipal properties is marginal (if found at all). This is not the case in North America where the loss of psychological status in being forced to move may be reinforced by a loss of credit worthiness.

The divergence between the 'economically best', and the 'socially best' solution to a problem is here apparent.

7 Renewal

Those areas undergoing spontaneous renewal are, however, not in the majority in most cities, since the criteria used by potential purchasers for property renovation are fairly demanding. Elsewhere, unless action is taken, normal property deterioration is likely to continue. Such action needs to be taken by national, state, or municipal government, and their degree of involvement depends itself on a number of fairly complex factors, notably finance, legal obligations and 'social conscience'.

Perhaps the minimum action that can be taken is where the municipal authority interferes *directly* in the land market. It has been suggested by various authors that since property taxation is part of the economic equation controlling urban change and decay, then changes in rate charges could be used to encourage spontaneous or desirable development. For example, Legler (1972) suggested:

... In recent years, the local real property tax system has come under increasing criticism. Concern has mounted over the inequities resulting from the way in which the system is generally administered as well as the apparent inability of property tax revenues to keep pace with the growing demand for more and better public services. In addition, the property tax has been denounced as a factor in the continued decline of our central cities. On the one hand, the proportionately lower tax rates in suburbia have undoubtedly played some part in encouraging out-migration. On the other hand, it is alleged that the fact that land and structures are taxed at the same rate discourages central city property owners from maintaining sound buildings or replacing derelict ones. Any incentive for improvement is negated by the threat of an increased tax bill. In response to these criticisms, proposals for property tax reform have focused not only on the financial and administrative aspects of property taxation but also on ways in which taxes can be used to promote socially desirable development goals. Taxes have come to be viewed as a technique for stimulating the redevelopment of our central cities as well as for collecting revenue.

Some who advocate the use of property taxes to encourage redevelopment assume that the need for planning and zoning will be reduced and that little or no public expense will be involved. For example:

... If we can change the rules of the game so that the players (investors) find it to their advantage to replace worn-out structures and develop land wisely, then there will be less need for restrictive measures such as zoning.

and that:

... For any particular property, the value of the tax exemption depends upon the spread between the tax rates on the land including improvements and the ratio of improved to total assessed value. Suppose two taxpayers own property assessed at $25,000. One has an improvement valued at $20,000 on land valued at $5,000. The other has an improvement valued at $10,000 on land valued at $15,000. Under a general property tax both would pay the same in taxes. If improvements were exempted altogether, the owner of the land valued at $15,000 would pay three times more in taxes than the owner of the land valued at $5,000. If the improvements were taxed at half their value under a graded tax, the owner of the $20,000 improvement would pay only three-quarters of the tax paid by the owner of the $10,000 improvement. By imposing a differentially higher tax on vacant or under-utilized land, a site value tax can make it unprofitable not to invest or redevelop. By investing in improvements, the owner can spread the fixed cost of the property tax over a greater income base. (Legler 1972)

In addition, Gaffney (1964) noted that at present property taxation tends towards the taxation of improvements rather than of decay, and argued that taxation should be heaviest on areas needing improvements rather than those that have been improved.

However, it must be obvious that such intervention is open to criticism. To start with taxation is only one part of the economic equation. By itself it is likely to have most effect in the marginal cases. Secondly, those most effected are likely to be the home owners – the remainder being able to pass on additional costs to the user. The owner occupier will be gradually forced out of the market, rents will tend to rise and the situation will be comparable to that arising from spontaneous redevelopment.

7.1 Renewal by public authorities: direct action

Direct action through renewal programmes have been in operation in the UK for the past fifty years. Between 1930 and 1939 over a third of a million slum properties were demolished in the UK alone, and in 1939 demolitions were taking place at 90,000 properties a year (Cullingworth 1972). In spite of the expenditure upon these, the number of properties needing demolition or action had increased markedly by 1946.

In the UK the deterioration during the war years, when capital for property improvements had been nearly absent, resulted in large inner city areas falling below normal standards of habitation. Bomb damage had extensively damaged other properties. (In much of Western Europe war damage had been severe within inner city areas. In North America an increasing awareness of property standards had been created by social stresses arising from the social upheaval of the war.)

Within the UK therefore, large areas of the inner cities were nearly 100 years old by 1946. This was important since much property was on 99 year leases, and it was expected that these would 'fall in' during the 1950s and early 1960s. The falling in of a lease means that the municipal authority can take possession of a property at a reasonable figure without going through the bother of buying through a compulsory purchase order. Planners and architects fired by a genuine social crusading zeal wished to provide better living conditions within cities and their idealism was bolstered by powers given under the 1947 Town and Country Planning Act, and through other Acts, including the 1946 New Towns Act.

However, redevelopment programmes could not start on a large scale in the immediate postwar period for three main reasons. Firstly, it takes time to design a programme of urban renewal. Secondly, war damage and an increasing population had created such a property shortage that further demolitions, even for only a short period, would only make the situation worse. Thirdly, finance was not available. Existing commitments in social services and education needed to be met first, and in the period of postwar austerity and adjustment central government finance was not available for large scale projects. The period of adjustment was lengthened by the Korean War.

The result was that large scale urban renewal programmes were not implemented in the UK until the 1950s. These developed from powers given to local authorities under the 1954 Act.

The advantages to the government of complete redevelopment were obvious. Firstly, large areas of cities were *ripe for development*. This meant that leases were simultaneously available within the city, that property had reached such a standard that demolition was the only possible solution, that schools and other facilities were outworn and in need of reconstruction anyway, and that underground services (gas, water, electricity, etc) were becoming inefficient and obsolete. In addition, new opportunities would be created by large scale clearances. The lumping together of individual properties (hereditaments) could create economically acceptable units for redevelopments. The total environment could be planned. Opportunities for new lines of communication to be constructed could be created, a more 'logical' distribution of land uses could be created within the city and non-conforming uses could be phased out.

There were, however, many problems facing municipal authorities. The operation of an urban renewal programme was obviously going to be complex. All properties needed to be incorporated individually. This meant large numbers of separate negotiations. In most cases owners had not wished to be involved, and it was necessary to invoke *compulsory purchase powers* to gain the property rights. Demolitions needed to be carried out and a new service infrastructure created. All of this needed to be done before redevelopment could start. Families and businesses who were dispossessed needed to be provided with temporary or permanent alternative accommodation.

Since one of the problems of such areas is overcrowding (with the resultant lowering of living standards) it can be seen that if areas are to be redeveloped at higher space standards per person, then it is difficult to rehouse as many people on the site. This meant that alternative development sites, on undeveloped land, needed to be found.

In many cases there was not the land available within the city's administrative area. This led to a hunt for land in other areas and to the construction of 'outcounty estates', with development partly paid for by one authority in the administrative area of another. Ground rules were laid down in the Town Development Act of 1952, and estates were constructed by the City of Manchester in Glossop, by the City of Liverpool in Kirby, and by the City of London at Haverhill, and Swindon. Some are contiguous with the city (eg Kirby), others are remote (eg Haverhill or Swindon). In other cases outcounty development took place as part of the new towns programmes of the UK.

Overriding all these was the problem of finance. Without money no programme could be started or completed. This was made available from central govern-ment in the form of grants to cover the major costs in urban renewal projects. But even with grants running up to seventy per cent the programme was still expensive for a municipal authority. So the minimization of those costs not grant covered would be a high priority, and one way in which costs can be kept down is to purchase leases at the date of reversion to the freeholder. At this date the user (lessee) has to vacate the property and the freeholder is responsible for all assets on the site. The authority needed only to negotiate with one person, ie the freeholder. At the same time, removal and other severance costs need not be borne by the authority since these costs would have had to be borne by the lessee in any case. In places this had led to redevelopment programmes taking place in phase with lease reversion and may account for what appears to be at first sight an arbitrary clearance programme.

In most cases, however, property rights needed to be compulsorily purchased. The compulsory acquisition of land by an authority was, until 1961, derived from the Land (Assessment of Compensation) Act of 1919, and the Town and Country Planning Acts of 1957 and 1959 (Part 1). Land was purchased at existing use value, with allowances made for disturbance. In 1961 the Land Compensation Act provided a fuller definition of compulsory purchase powers (Heap 1972).

Land could be bought for necessary purposes (including redevelopment) at market value, but this value should not include any increase deriving from the municipal programme of improvements. This prevented the owner benefiting from the expenditure of municipal finance. Also the owner could not gain from increased values in any unaffected but contiguous land holdings. The increase in value of one must be set off against the other. Various moving expenses are incorporated. The change from *existing use* to *market value* in 1961 as a basis for assessment markedly increased the cost of land to the renewal authority, and special provisions were built into the act. Properties declared 'slums' could be purchased at site value or at a minimum equal to the gross rateable value of the site and property. In inner city areas this was often as low as £5 or £10 per property. Since the 1969 Act, however, the owner occupier has been able to obtain full market value for his property, but the definition in relation to rented accommodation remains as above.

In the UK a house is a 'slum' and defined as being unfit for human habitation if '*it is so far defective in one or more of the said matters that it is not reasonably suitable for occupation in that condition*'. The 'said matters' are:

1 repair
2 stability
3 freedom from damp
4 natural lighting
5 ventilation
6 water supply
7 drainage and sanitary conveniences
8 facilities for the preparation of cooking of food and for the disposal of waste water

This is a statutory list, see Housing Act 1957, Part II (5.4), and action *may* be taken in respect of poor internal arrangements (Circular No. 69/67, para 3, Part IV).

Such a definition leaves considerable scope to the individual judgement of the public health inspector or valuer, and has led to many objections and complaints that land is being 'got on the cheap'.

Dennis (1973) in his book describing the urban renewal programmes of the Millfield area of Sunderland argues that the normal definition is far too limited and rates conformity higher than diversity. He concludes:

... In a bureaucracy of consumption, which local planning authorities are in their clearance and improvement schemes, everything depends upon the visibility and uniformity of the values at stake in what is being consumed ... if values are obvious and uncontroversial, the bureaucracy can supply its criteria and deliver accurate descriptions of cases falling below approved levels. But when the values are heterogeneous and opaque to the bureaucracy, it is essential that those whose values are being affected, in this case the consumers of housing, should find maximum scope for the expression of their preferences and that these preferences should be seriously considered as data: the wish to be rehoused by the Council, the wish to modernize, the wish to be left alone. (Dennis 1973)

Comprehensive renewal provides both social opportunities and social problems. Opportunities are created in that existing inhabitants are found accommodation at standards well above the minimum (at Parker Morris Standards in the UK) in areas that are modern, and (hopefully) well planned. Problems arise from the dislocation created by complete clearance and redevelopment. Firstly, individuals may feel a direct economic loss due to the compulsory purchase of their property, and a psychological loss in the destruction of their previous physical environment. More serious is the direct social disorganization. Families will be moved and rehoused as the demolition programme takes place. Neighbour and family relationships may be fragmented, especially if the receiving areas for the population to be rehoused are far away. Some disruption is inevitable even where a maximum of care is taken by the municipal body, a disruption that will tend to be worse for the elderly than for the young. The existing community will be destroyed, and it is unlikely to be recreated elsewhere.

Such disorientation and dislocation is in many ways worse within North America where municipal rehousing commitments are in most cases absent. For example, Hartman (1964) made a study of the housing of families relocated from West End, Boston. His survey found that families tended to find accommodation of a slightly higher standard than those of West End, but that families were forced into paying more to achieve this higher standard.

Hartman concluded that

... Although the results of forced relocation appear to vary widely from project to project, on the whole relocation has made a disappointingly small contribution to the attainment of 'a decent home in a suitable living environment for every American family'. Given the premise that one of the cardinal aims of renewal and rehousing should be the improved housing welfare of those living in substandard conditions, it is questionable whether the limited and inconsistent gains reported in most studies represent an acceptable level of achievement. Not only have the gains been limited, but they have been accompanied by widespread increases in housing costs, often incurred irrespective of an improvement in housing or the ability or desire to absorb these costs. In most clearance areas, some degree of improvement is inevitable, since people are being moved from marginal or substandard sections. (As the Chicago Housing Authority observed, 'It would have been difficult for families occupying the sites to have found a worse segment of the city's housing than the one they had occupied'.) The real questions for public policy have to do with the degree of improvement the community should demand from rehousing operations and the nature of the rules imposed.

It is an inescapable conclusion that relocation has been only an ancillary component of the renewal process; were this not the case, the community would find totally unacceptable 'slum clearance' projects which leave as many as two-thirds of the displaced families all living in substandard conditions, or which actually increase the incidence of overcrowding. With few exceptions, relocation in this country has not truly been *a rehousing effort* (in the British sense of the word), a plan which focuses

Table 7 Relocation destinations of West End sample

Distance from West End in miles	(1) Number	(2) Percent	(3) Number dwelling units in each 1-mile ring	%	(4) Expected number of re-locatees within 6-mile radius	(5) Index of dispersion (1) ÷ (4)
0–1	91	17	21,000	5	23	3.96
1–2	89	17	61,000	16	73	1.22
2–3	86	16	73,000	19	87	0.99
3–4	78	15	87,000	23	106	0.74
4–5	76	14	87,000	23	106	0.73
5–6	39	7	55,000	14	64	0.61
	(459)		384,000	100	459	

Source: Hartman (1964)

Table 8 Distribution of pre- and post-relocation rent income ratios, West End sample

Rent/income ratio	West End %	Post-relocation %
Less than 5.0%	3	0
5.0–9.9%	18	7
10.0–14.9%	42	23
15.0–19.9%	17	28
20.0–24.9%	10	19
25.0–29.9%	1	9
30.0–39.9%	6	8
40% or more	3	6
	100	100
Medium rent/income ratio	13.6%	18.6%

Source: Hartman (1964)

primary attention on the problem of how to insure that people living in substandard housing are settled into decent homes. In city after city, one sees that the great amount of time and effort spent in investigation and condemning housing conditions in the slums that local authorities wish to tear down is in no sense matched by corresponding public and professional interest in the fate of displaced families once they have been dislodged. It is perhaps revealing to note that only one-half of one per cent of the $2.2 billion of gross project costs for all Federal aided urban renewal projects (through 1960) was spent on relocation. (Hartman 1964)

For a period of perhaps ten years before redevelopment, neighbourhoods will tend to become progressively more blighted. This problem was well spotlighted by Stones (1972) when he argued that the problem is bad enough if redevelopment is taking place rapidly, but in a city like Liverpool where redevelopment has been halted (since demolition has taken place faster than architects and planners can redevelop the sites), things are made far worse. Though physical redevelopment might stop, physical, economic and social decay will not.

We have concentrated very much upon residential redevelopment within this section. However, it is as well to remember that all forms of land use are involved in any *comprehensive redevelopment* project. That is to say in a project in which the whole area is cleared, replanned and reconstructed from scratch. If such a scheme is to be planned with a minimum of constraints it is necessary for *all* uses to be cleared. The presence of even one large existing user may well prevent the full use being made of the opportunity created by the clearance. Industrial and commercial properties may therefore be forced into redevelopment, and the problems facing the businessman and his business are as complex as those of the owner occupier or landlord.

For example, local service facilities (shops, etc.) will become increasingly uneconomic as their markets (the local residential population) move away. At present the owner does not have a right to claim compensation for such blighting. An ethical problem is raised. We have already noted the rationale that no-one should profit by the action of government in urban renewal. Should an owner be also allowed to lose? The question of compensation in such a case has not been satisfactorily resolved.

Businesses will find that their employees are moving away. Wage demands are likely to increase as employees are affected by increased housing and commuting costs. The owners of those businesses affected by compulsory purchase will need to invest time and money searching for new premises. Berry (1968) estimates that in the United States some 120,000 businesses were displaced between 1949 and 1968. Of these one in every three was unable to face moving and went into liquidation. In a study of Hyde Park-Kenwood (Chicago) he found that the mortality rates of such businesses faced by renewal programmes was higher than normally expected, though he also concluded that many such businesses would have gone into liquidation within the near future anyway. Similar conclusions were reached by Townroe (1971), though he tended to think that disruption could also affect the long term viability of businesses, unless new opportunities were created.

One problem is that cheap industrial and business premises within the inner city have traditionally provided a base within which new industrial firms could start. Without such a property reservoir the number of new commercial organizations starting business may well fall. Birmingham has recognized this and attempted to provide new low cost commercial property for such small businesses. What cannot be recreated, however, are areas with businesses existing in symbiosis, or with very close contractual relationships.

Once an area has been cleared of existing development it is possible to begin reconstruction. The design process will hopefully have been undertaken whilst the clearance was underway. Opportunities for new communication links, for the removal of non-conforming industry and for the reorganization of commercial facilities within the city will have been taken into account. In many cases complete city centre redevelopment is linked to a general urban renewal programme.

In relation to residential property the municipal authority has had a series of policy decisions to take. The most important of these is to decide upon the density standards of the new development. Densities in multiple-used inner city areas are in many cases 250 persons per acre, and in Glasgow densities of 500 persons per acre have been recorded (Jephcott 1972). After taking into account the provision of new communications and services, the area available for residential property will be reduced. If space standards per person are to be higher than in the original state (including things like localized play areas and gardens) then either the new development will not contain the same number of people as the old, or buildings must be higher thereby allowing vertical rather than horizontal use.

The choice between these alternatives has varied from city to city, and from area to area within a city depending largely upon the date of the decision. In economic terms the choice lies between two separate sets of costs. *High rise development* (up to 200 persons per acre) is extremely expensive to construct even taking into account generous government assistance, largely because of lifts and fire precautions. It uses less land than other development, though this gain is less than might be expected since parking, playing and daylighting areas depend upon the population and building size and do not vary directly with density. Lichfield (1959) estimates that high rise development is economically feasible only where land prices are extremely high, though this view is contradicted by Jensen (1966).

The advantages of such development are that the municipal authority gains in rateable values since it retains as large a number of residences in its own area as possible, and needs to provide few facilities in outcounty areas. It retains a high population for local employment, and provides a large market for its CBD and other facilities. It provides residential accommodation near to the centre of the city, and minimizes personal commuting costs. In many cases, Glasgow for example, this form of development has been chosen. For example, between July 1968 and May 1969, twenty new high rise apartment blocks were built to join the 143 already in existence.

Figure 7 Multi-storey apartment blocks in Glasgow, 1968 and 1969 Source: Jephcott (1972)

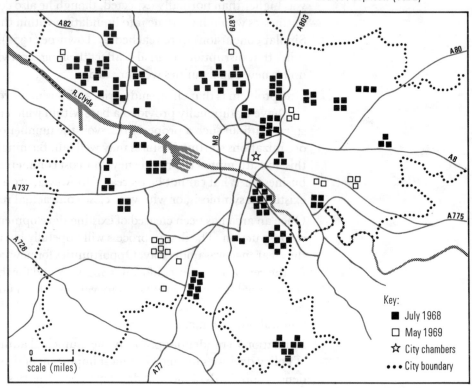

There are some economic problems, however. It is impossible to charge economic rents for such property. Since, for example, it is estimated that in central London the cost of a three bedroomed flat may be in excess of £15,000, with an economic rent of £20 per week. If low income families are to use such property some subsidy is needed, and the present government policy is to encourage market-rent letting. Social problems may be intense. Disorientation created by living in high flats, vandalism, the absence of play areas and the loss of the human scale are all well documented problems. Jephcott (1972) has described the whole problem in great detail in respect of Glasgow, and has also described the rapid decline in housing standards in high rise development. She also makes the point that some families will accept these things. Many of them came perhaps from the Gorbals and other private tenement areas and were used to high density living. Such problems may therefore be less important in areas where high rise developments have been accepted over a longer period or where alternatives do not exist, for example, near Stockholm, Paris or Warsaw.

It has been argued that human scale can be retained with very high density dwellings without the need for high rise property. One such attempt has been made in Sheffield. The Park Hill estate has been redeveloped at similar densities to the original. This type of development still reduces the human scale however, and there is no evidence to suggest that such development is more acceptable than high rise construction *per se*.

Plate 4 High density redevelopment

The second major alternative is to construct at lower densities with low rise property, ie property of three stories or less. This is cheaper to construct, but provides less accommodation. It creates a land demand elsewhere, and leads to those outcounty problems described earlier. Aesthetically from the outside it is less acceptable, though internally it is perhaps more satisfactory.

One problem not foreseen in clearance programmes, however, has been the greater demand for replacement property within the UK than originally estimated. There is an undertaking for clearance authorities to rehouse some of those dispossessed by their programmes, and in many cases these have taken up their option to do so. Also many families not on the municipal lists as needing municipal accommodation have, upon demolition, applied for municipal housing. In North and South American cities no such undertaking or facility exists. Once an area is cleared, families who are not eligible for municipal housing must move on and find other private property. This can increase pressures elsewhere within the city, and the whole process creates the same types of problems as spontaneous redevelopment.

Keyes (1969) suggests that in many American cities this lack of a commitment to rehouse has been deliberately used to the advantage of a sectarian policy. If the local political framework is controlled by middle class legislators a desire to renew the city can be expressed by a deliberate policy to exclude the poor and underprivileged (as well as those engaged in the seamier activities of society), and to disrupt what are regarded as undesirable subcultures. The process is analogous to the moving on of vagrants by the police, only here the under-privileged are forced to move on by the removal of their physical environment.

It is not surprising that in some areas municipalities have found it advisable to construct properties for sale within clearance areas. These can be sold at economic prices, and the profits used to provide municipal services, but it does mean a banishment of the poorer members of the community from some of the inner city areas.

Comprehensive urban renewal is thus a large scale operation involving a complex procedure, taking time and money. If anything is lacking for the smooth running of the operation, then problems may result. Some of these have been described by Stones (1972), in far more detail by Keyes (1969) in relation to Boston, Mass., as noted earlier in this unit.

In order to phase development, the municipal authority in the UK has powers (under the 1954 Act) to purchase property and defer demolition until the whole scheme is ready. It is not a popular power since necessary renovation must be carried out in the short term, and most authorities do not wish to gain a reputation as slum landlords. It can, however, be useful when parts only of a redevelopment area can be purchased at any one time and when the municipal authority wishes to limit its rehousing commitments. It is perhaps most useful when property is not yet in need of clearance, but where clearance in the longer term will be of benefit to a larger clearance area.

The designation of certain clearance and renewal areas may stem less from the state of the buildings within the areas than from the need to use the land for other purposes. For example, on the one hand the construction of inner city ring roads may result from the opportunities created by urban renewal. It may also create the possibility of using urban renewal funds to clear a site for such new roads. Land purchased for such renewal using state or local funds means that this land is relatively cheap to a municipal authority. Local inhabitants are not likely to be particularly articulate, and able to resist. Keyes has shown how such opportunities have been used in North America, where no require-ment exists to move dispossessed families or businesses, and where urban renewal funds can be used in effect to subsidize transport undertakings. There is no reason to assume that this policy has not been followed within the UK. More recently, however, the advantages of this sort of undertaking have become less marked since a new militancy has been created amongst inner city dwellers, especially in negro areas in the United States.

8 Rehabilitation

During the 1950s it was apparent that, taking into account the funds available for urban renewal, urban decay could not be eradicated in the foreseeable future. At the same time social problems arising from earlier renewal programmes were becoming apparent. Various interested parties were feeling that the comprehensive policies were too all-embracing. Although published later, the pent-up frustration of these is expressed by McKee (1971) when he describes the comprehensive redevelopment process as one resulting from the 'Whitehall Bulldozer'. The main frustration stemmed from the way in which municipalities could redevelop areas if they could show that it was *reasonable*, not that it was *impossible to do otherwise*. That is to say the local authority needed only to show the properties were in a poor state and that redevelopment was possible. They did not have to prove that alternatives to redevelopment had been investigated and that it was concluded that these were not feasible. Redevelopment just had to be *one* of the alternatives, not that it had to be the best.

As an alternative to direct action, a housing improvement policy had been introduced in 1949, but really only implemented in 1954/5. Under this individuals could get grants to upgrade the state of individual properties and raise standards by the provision of new facilities. In 1959 the present system of standard and discretionary grants was introduced. These grants were for individual properties and allowed structural renovation as well as the provision of facilities. Over time the exact amount of the grant has varied, but is usually within the region of fifty per cent of the cost of renovation, to a maximum value of £1,000.

It has been argued that this retains as many of the individuals within an inner city area as possible, and prevents the undesirable breakup of family properties into multiple use. In effect it decreases renovation costs on buildings to the owner, and thus allows him to bring it closer to modern tastes and needs. It therefore encourages 'spontaneous' redevelopment by reducing conversion and modification costs. It has also been argued that it encouraged speculation in the land market at times of intense property demands since it acts as a £1,000 gift to a developer.

In 1969, however, the situation was changed by the 1969 Housing Acts. Under these, grants could be given for area rehabilitation as well as for individual properties. Prior to this date municipalities had, in some cases, decided that certain zones within a slum clearance area could be made useful by the addition of capital. For example, if the properties were structurally sound and space provision was viable, then modifications could recreate a community in human scale. To do this the municipality could claim grants for individual properties (eg the Deeplish areas of Rochdale) but had to bear environmental costs from their own funds. Since 1969 it has been possible to rehabilitate whole areas by retaining the existing infrastructure and to get finance for the operation as a whole including environmental work. Development can be retained at a human scale, and costs kept as low as possible (Moore 1972).

To gain an understanding of the type of scheme that is now possible under the 1969 Act it is worthwhile to refer to the city of Norwich where the 1961 census showed that of the 40,031 dwellings in the city at that time, 13,560 did not have the exclusive use of one or more of the following basic amenities – a water closet, fixed bath and hot and cold water. Since that time approximately 3,700 houses have either been demolished or included for demolition in the council's slum clearance programme and, up to the end of 1968, 2,060 houses have had improvement grants. The yearly rate of improvement has increased from 129 in 1961 to 345 in 1968, but even so it will take some twenty years to improve the remaining houses, during which time many will have become unfit.

It was decided that improvement schemes for a number of areas ringing the city centre should be investigated. The first of these should be the Arlington area – a compact half-mile zone of housing about half a mile to the south-west of the city centre (Figure 8).

The area contained 1,500 dwellings, mainly in long terraces. Of these approximately 750 have the basic amenities, but only 221 had previously received improvement grants. Of the remainder, 86 properties were classified as slums and have since been demolished. Using improvement grants, and general amenity grants the city council decided firstly to upgrade the physical living conditions of the area. All householders were encouraged to obtain grants. To date 1,150 out of 1,400 eligible householders have done so. An investigation into the remaining 250 is underway. At the same time new sewers and other services have been provided to improve the area's infrastructure. The plan itself proposes that through traffic should be prevented by the blocking of streets to cars, and that the resultant open areas should be landscaped.

Figure 8 The Arlington scheme Source: City Planning Office, Norwich

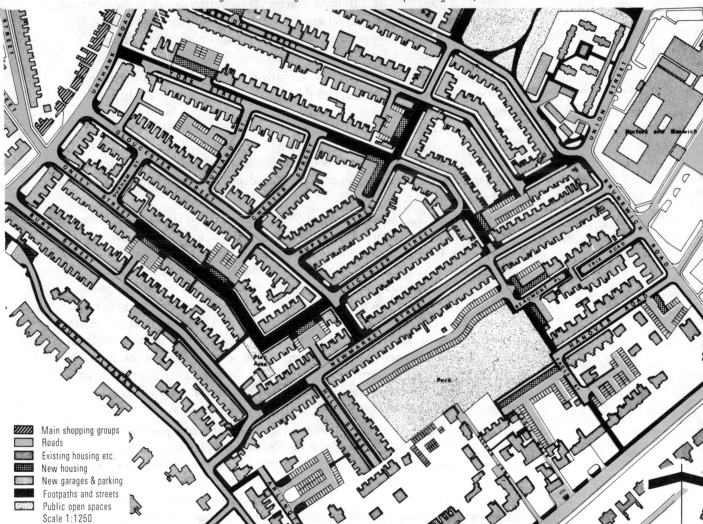

Main shopping groups
Roads
Existing housing etc.
New housing
New garages & parking
Footpaths and streets
Public open spaces
Scale 1:1250

It is the intention of the scheme to provide off street parking, so that on its completion in 1974 a whole inner city area will consist of houses of a reasonable standard, with an improved internal and external environment.

The total cost of the project was estimated in 1969 at £576,849, when all grants have been taken into account, ie a cost of £600 per house. This compares favourably with those costs that would have been incurred in a full scale redevelopment, and it appears that this disparity between improvement and renewal is fairly normal. When comparing the two, however, as will be done later in this unit you should remember that there are still problems.

Firstly, such a solution is short term. Even after improvements have been carried out the property is not as satisfactory as purpose built modern housing in terms of the internal ordering of space, insulation and servicing. It has been estimated that the life of such improvements is perhaps fifteen years, so this means that in fifteen years the problem may need to be faced again.

Secondly, this type of area rehabilitation applies mainly to single family units. The problems resulting from multiple occupation are not eased, and if it

Plates 5, 6, 7 A series of three photographs showing an area prior to redevelopment, and post-redevelopment

becomes worthwhile to reconvert to single property units may even be worsened. Thirdly, in order to increase space standards it may be necessary to demolish certain properties, to phase others out of use so as to use the space for the remainder, or to provide off street car parking or open space. These will tend to reduce the size of population living within the area, and still present the authority with a rehousing problem.

Finally, it would appear that for such a scheme to be put into operation it is often necessary to persuade the local authority to take on the extra work involved in administering such a scheme. The reluctance of local authorities to take action has been reflected in the increasing activism of community action groups concerned with disseminating information to residents about grant availability and their rights, and with providing a pressure point to encourage governmental action. This type of activism is well documented in the work of Goodman (1972) and Dennis (1973).

9 Urban renewal or rehabilitation

Between 1955 and 1970 some 1,153,591 properties were demolished or closed to be demolished as slums in the United Kingdom. In the same period 1,664,691 properties received improvement grants. As can be seen from Table 9, clearances were taking place in the UK at just under 90,000 per year by 1970. Improvement grants were 179,957 in 1970, and since then the numbers appear to have risen still further. It is now intended that a minimum of 200,000 dwellings should be rehabilitated and improved annually. Even with this rate of renewal, however, Buchanan (1972) estimates that there will still be a back-log of inner city properties in need of renewal, and by the year 2000 this will include products of the earlier periods of urban renewal.

Table 9 Slum clearance and improvement 1955–70

	Slum clearance			Improvements		
	England and Wales	Scotland	Great Britain	England and Wales	Scotland	Great Britain
1955–9	213,402	61,545	274,947	219,068	16,051	235,119
1960–4	303,621	62,569	366,190	610,778	21,989	632,767
1965	60,666	15,534	76,200	122,993	6,333	129,326
1966	66,782	16,650	83,432	107,720	7,569	115,289
1967	71,152	19,087	90,239	113,142	7,307	120,449
1968	71,586	18,768	90,354	114,216	13,679	127,895
1969	69,233	17,847	87,080	108,938	14,951	123,889
1970	67,804	17,345	85,149	156,557	23,400	179,957
Total 1955–70	924,246	229,345	1,153,591	1,553,412	111,279	1,664,691

Source: Cullingworth (1972) p 267

It is often thought that *urban renewal* and *urban rehabilitation* are two distinct solutions to the problems facing the inner area. The proponents of urban renewal argue that it is the only way in which the opportunities of the inner city can be properly exploited. That it is the only way in which land can be used efficiently, and that past social problems are the result of poor design and phasing which can be overcome with better planning procedures. Detractors argue that it is wasteful in resources, that either new urban slums are created or social disorientation is created, that for long periods urban deserts are created, that it is of inhuman scale and that conformity has replaced diversity. Proponents of urban rehabilitation argue that a social life can be retained, that the human scale and diversity are retained and that change is not necessarily for the better. Detractors argue that rehabilitation still displaces people and businesses, that the favoured few alone profit and that these few are often not typical of the problem, that opportunities are lost, that an

Plate 8 The Arlington Scheme: selective clearance for redevelopment

Plate 9 The Arlington Scheme: structural and building renovation

inefficient nineteenth century land use pattern is reinforced in twentieth century cities, and that in effect planning is for the present and not the future.

Of course, most of these arguments revolve about direct economic costs, and if we return to the Arlington scheme we can see why this has been so. It was estimated by the city that for the 1,400 houses in Arlington, local authority costs would be £40,000 higher for improvement than for complete renewal, but that the saving to central government for improvement would be £350,000. This was derived from the calculations shown in Tables 10 and 11.

Table 10 Relative costs of renewal (Scheme 1) and improvement (Scheme 2) to a local authority

Scheme 1	Cost £	Scheme 2	Cost £
Redevelopment in 15 years (acquisition less appropriation)	518,037	Redevelopment in 40 years (acquisition less appropriation)	152,934
Improvement expenditure now	74,300	Improvement expenditure now	482,110
	592,337		635,044

Table 11 Relative costs of renewal (Scheme 1) and improvement (Scheme 2) to central government

Scheme 1	£	Scheme 2	£
Net cost subsidies for redevelopment over 15 years	860,000	Net cost subsidies for redevelopment in 40 years	256,000
Grants given now	222,900	Grants given now	489,211
	1,082,900		745,211
Assumes a 10% discount rate			

Source: *The Arlington Scheme*, Norwich City Council, 1969

Therefore it is directly cheaper to improve rather than renew, but as has been pointed out earlier, it may not eradicate all the problems, and may be staving off long term problems for a short term gain.

Since tastes and aspirations are continually changing there appears to be no end to the need for some type of renewal process within the city, but whether existing policies, or the absence of policies, are carrying out changes to the benefit of the community is open to doubt.

If you look at who gains and loses from urban decay and renewal it can be seen that the owner and municipal authorities tend to gain most, and the dweller or user least. The owner gains from increased values and grants, the municipal authority from increased land values resulting from purchase and renewal. The dweller gains where he is rehoused successfully. In many cases, however, the person in multiple occupation with minimal facilities gains little. He may not be rehoused, he gains only marginally from improvements and his competitive position within the property market is continually worsened at a time when land values are rising.

Urban renewal has always reflected building and environmental standards, and is concerned with land. The basic problems facing the inner city are the result of market imperfections, especially in relation to the lack of capital, that is to say of poverty. The lack of capital in relation to property conditions can be ameliorated by clearance projects. Poverty, in terms of the ability of individuals to purchase an environment fit to live in, has not been eradicated, or even its eradication aimed at directly. There is little point in redeveloping the inner city if the inhabitants of this area cannot be rehoused at a level they can afford. Perhaps it might be cheaper to attack poverty from the other end and pay income at a high enough level for renewal to take place without quite so many visible signs of the 'bulldozer', ie to allow the poor to choose where they wish to live.

However, the final choice will be made not in relation to some nebulous concept of 'rightness' but through the interaction of four groups of people: the owners of inner city land; the users of this land; technical planners; and politicians. A possible way of modelling their interaction is made by Wolpert (1972) in the paper, 'Possible ways of viewing neighbourhood change' reprinted in Supplementary Material. It is probably worthwhile reading this paper now to put various points made in the unit into another perspective. The relative strengths of these groups in society will determine whether urban renewal is dominated by the needs of market efficiency, social equity, people or buildings. Our future city is going to depend upon the actions of today, and a study of these actions suggests that conflicting interests will ensure that no single course of action will be taken to renew and revitalize the inner city.

A guide to further reading

The amount of further reading that could be done on the topic is very large indeed. This reflects an increasing awareness by the academic, researcher, planner and politician of the problems of decaying inner cities. A number of references in the set books have been referred to in this text. In addition D. HARVEY (1971) 'Social processes, spatial form and the redistribution of real income in an urban system' in M. STEWART (ed) (1972) *The City*, provides a useful, though not completely neutral, approach to the whole concept of equity within the inner city.

For those who wish to investigate the economic aspects of the urban development and redevelopment process, B. GOODALL (1972) *The Economics of Urban Areas*, Pergamon, provides a useful text. On the other hand R. GOODMAN (1972) *After the Planners*, Penguin, presents an extremely powerful attack on the use of any form of economic evaluation within the urban renewal process. The author argues strongly that social costs so outweigh economic benefits that the latter could be ignored by society. Using a different approach in L. KEYS (1969)

The rehabilitation planning game, MIT Press, the way in which the need to prove an economic viability for a project may be used to ensure that inequitable policies, are carried out is described. In J. MCKEE (1971) *The Whitehall Bulldozer*, Hobart Paper, there is an attack on the whole principle of urban renewal, in which arguments similar to those of Keys are spelt out in detail.

The question of whether redevelopment should be at high or low density has recently been much discussed. An analysis of these arguments is well carried out in P. JEPHCOTT (1972) *Homes in High Flats*, Oliver and Boyd. In S. PEPPER (1971) *Housing Improvement: Goals and Strategy*, Lund Humphries, the scale of the problem in the United Kingdom is described and alternatives are discussed. The author includes a fairly detailed costing analysis of a renewal scheme for Leeds that is, perhaps, quite well worth comparing with that of the Arlington Scheme in Norwich, included in the text.

For those of you particularly interested in the potential impact of redevelopment schemes upon local residents then a study of N. DENNIS (1972) *Public Participation and Planners' Blight*, Faber and Faber, might prove useful. In this he describes the whole redevelopment process in Millfield (Sunderland), and discusses the way in which *Gemeinschaft* developed in response to the threat of redevelopment. You might well feel after reading the book that there is no hope for direct public participation in the process. Bureaucracy is too dominant. If you feel this, then perhaps you should refer back to JEPHCOTT (1972) to see that there are two sides to this problem, ie resistance can negate even beneficial policies.

All of these references constitute optional extra reading for those who wish to extend themselves in a particular direction. You should be able to achieve the objectives within this unit by reference to the main text and to the associated reading. When completing this unit you should be able to analyse the various statements being made about this very live issue in an unbiased way, so that you can appreciate why society's freedom of action in relation to urban decay is constrained, and why the problem has not been yet successfully solved.

Self-assessment questions

SAQ 1   What would happen to the value of a property (not site) if it was to depreciate at 3% per annum through age, but increase in value by 1% per annum through inflation, over a 50 year period. The property was originally valued at £10,000 when constructed, and after 15 years the owner spent £1,000 on renovating it. What would it be worth in 35 years after construction?

SAQ 2   Whinston and Davis (1961) have suggested that except for mistaken judgement profit maximization should take place. What sort of factors could mistaken judgement cover?

SAQ 3   Changes in tastes have led to older properties becoming unsuitable as dwelling places for the economically more affluent and discerning. List the major demands for internal improvements in properties that have taken place over the past seventy years.

SAQ 4   The ability of the property owner to maximize on his site is limited by several factors, that have been termed a property trap. What are these limitations?

SAQ 5   If a property owner cannot demolish his property and redevelop with a more profitable use within the inner city, what is the most likely thing he will do if he has sufficient capital?

SAQ 6   In spontaneous urban renewal, changes in an area's social structure are likely to occur. What are these?

SAQ 7   What are the main advantages to the municipal authority of comprehensive urban renewal schemes?

SAQ 8   From your reading of the unit what do you think is meant by *ripe for development*?

SAQ 9   Within an urban renewal scheme, who is eligible for compensation and rehousing in an entirely residential area in the United Kingdom and the United States?

SAQ 10   When comparing comprehensive renewal and area rehabilitation it is often said that the former involves greater short term costs and that the latter will incur more in the long term. List the types of short term costs to be borne by the municipal authority in both alternatives.

SAQ 11   List the advantages and disadvantages that various authors have ascribed to high rise inner city development.

SAQ 12   During the period 1955 to 1970 there has been a major change in government policy in relation to housing renewal or improvement in the United Kingdom. Using data from the unit describe this change.

Answers to SAQs

Answer SAQ 1   You must remember that the depreciation involves a compound calculation and that the true depreciation will be 3–1% per annum, ie 2%. Thus a building worth £10,000 in year A will be worth £7,386 in year A + 15, that is 15 years after construction. If £1,000 is then added to the value then its true worth in year A + 15 will be £8,386, and after 35 years it will be worth £5,627. You should note that no allowance has been made for inflation, and therefore all figures are in 'A' values.

Answer SAQ 2   The types of factors one would find under 'mistaken judgement' would be: that the owner does not know his true site value, does not know his true property value, is not aware of his true position of profitability, is not able to understand what is going to happen in relation to either the demand or supply of his type of property, does not know about the availability of finance for improvement, or is not aware of the returns he could get by investing in other things.

Answer SAQ 3   Obviously many trends have created changes in housing aspirations. The most obvious would be:

a Increasing demand for individual space, shown through demands, for example, for separate bedrooms for all family members.

b Increasing use of domestic equipment, refrigerators, washing machines, etc, creating more space demands in kitchen.

c Increasing demands for hot water throughout the house.

d Demands for central heating, and double glazing.

e Demands for electrical power in all parts of the house.

f The need to have integral sanitary facilities.

g The demand for on site or integral car parking.

h A decline in the availability of servants resulting in an increasing search for household efficiency.

Answer SAQ 4   A property owner's ability to maximize on his site value is limited by legal, financial and planning constraints, as well as by lack of knowledge of his own potential.

Answer SAQ 5   If a property owner has the inclination and finance to develop his property, but is constrained by planning or legal constraints, then he will try to operate in those areas where he is least affected. He might therefore try to improve his property internally so that he can charge higher rents and get a higher return on his capital. He might alter the internal structure so that he can increase income by introducing multiple occupation (although in the United Kingdom this has become more difficult in recent years through the extension of planning legislation).

Answer SAQ 6   The main changes would tend to be the immigration of families or households able to pay the higher rents, or purchase values, and the enforced emigration of lower income groups. Middle class colonization could result.

Answer SAQ 7   The main advantages are:

a Administrative convenience

b Financial incentives

c Economies of scale

d Increased receipts upon completion

Answer SAQ 8   An area that is ripe for development is one in which leases are simultaneously available, has a high proportion of (technically) slum property, shows signs of environmental decay, services are inefficient, and in planning terms is becoming a centre of social deviation.

Answer SAQ 9   In the United Kingdom all residents whether owners, occupiers or lodgers are eligible for rehousing. Compensation is limited to those with a legal interest within the site, ie owners and lessees. In the United States there is in most cases, no obligation to rehouse, though municipal housing *may* be offered. Compensation arrangements are, however, the same as for the United Kingdom.

Answer SAQ 10   A listing could be made in tabular form as follows:

	Renewal	Rehabilitation
Demolition	large scale	limited
Compensation	large scale	limited
Services	large scale	medium scale
Construction	large scale	limited
Improvements	small	large scale

Answer SAQ 11   The advantages of high rise development have been variously described as cleanliness, privacy, proximity to services and employment, administratively sensible, externally aesthetically pleasant, the ability to rehouse large numbers of the original inhabitants locally, and the possibility of producing inner city 'green areas'.

The disadvantages have been described as social disorientation, noise and lack of privacy, soullessness, the inability of mothers to allow children to play outside, the lack of individuality and of human scale, and the high initial expenditure. Other criticisms have been made in relation to Ronan Point (following its collapse), but these are really specific to a type of construction rather than about the concept of high rise development.

Answer SAQ 12   To answer this you should refer to Table 9. Firstly, you should note that although the numbers of slum clearances and improvements have increased slightly year by year until 1970, the balance has changed considerably. In the period 1955–8, the numbers under each heading were approximately equal, that in the period 1960–5 improvements were being carried out at a rate double that of slum clearances, and that by 1970 this disparity had increased even more.

One can link this data to the changes in government policy as shown in the 1954 Act, and the 1969 Act. This leads to a conclusion that comprehensive slum clearance is becoming less attractive to government as time goes on. It could of course also be explained if those areas of cities in *obvious* need of renovation have now been cleared and the major areas remaining are in *need* of improvement rather than complete clearance and redevelopment.

References   ALONSO, W. (1964) *Location and land use*, MIT Press.

BERRY, B. J. (1968) *The impact of urban renewal on small businesses*, Center for Studies, University of Chicago.

BOURNE, L. S. (ed) (1971) *Internal Structure of the City*, Oxford University Press (set book).

BUCHANAN, C. (1972) *The prospect for housing*, Nationwide Building Society.

CLARKE, B. (1972). 'Rural urban relationships with special reference to Crawley New Town', in *Geographica Polonica*, 4, 1972.

CULLINGWORTH, J. and WATSON, C. J. (1972) *Housing in Clydeside*, Reports on a household survey and a housing condition survey in the Central Clydeside Conurbation, HMSO.

CULLINGWORTH, J. (1963) *Housing in transition*, Heinemann.

CULLINGWORTH, J. (1972) *Town and Country Planning in Britain*, George Allen and Unwin.

DENNIS, N. (1972) *Public Participation and Planners' Blight*, Faber and Faber.

GAFFNEY, M. M. (1964) 'Property taxes and the frequency of urban renewal' in *Proceedings* of the fifty-seventh national tax conference, Pittsburgh, Pennsylvania, September 1964.

GOODALL, B. (1972) *The economics of urban areas*, Pergamon Press.

GOODMAN, R. (1972) *After the Planners*, Penguin.

GRAY, P. G. and RUSSELL, R. (1962) *The housing situation in 1960*, HMSO.

HABBERTON, J. (1889) 'Our Cities' in STRAUSS, A. (ed) (1968) *The American City*, Allen Lane, pp 134–40.

HARTMAN, C. (1964) 'The housing of relocated families' in *Journal of the American Institute of Planners*, 30, 4, pp 266–86; reprinted in WILSON, J. (ed) (1966) *Urban Renewal*, MIT Press, pp 293–335.

HEAP, D. (1972) *An outline of planning law*, Sweet and Maxwell.

JAMES, P. (1962) *An introduction to English law*, Butterworth.

JENSEN, R. (1966) *High density living*, Leonard Hill.

JEPHCOTT, P. (1972) *Homes in High Flats*, Oliver and Boyd.

KEYS, L. (1969) *The rehabilitation planning game*, MIT Press.

KIRWAN, R. M. and MARTIN, D. B. (1972) *The economics of urban residential renewal and improvement*, Centre for Environmental Studies, CES WP 77.

LEGLER, J. (1972) 'Alternative forms of property taxation as a stimulus to urban redevelopment' in *American Society of Planning Officials Year Book, 1971*, pp 157–68.

LEYHAUSEN, P. (1965) 'The same community – a density problem', in *Discovery*, September 1965.

LICHFIELD, N. (1959) *Economics of planned development*. Estates Gazette.

MCHARG, I. (1969) *Design with nature*, Doubleday Press.

MCHARG, I. (1972) *Losing out*, Notting Hill Peoples Association Housing Group.

MCKEE, J. (1971) *The Whitehall Bulldozer*, Institute of Economic Affairs, Hobart Paper No 52.

MOORE, R. (1972) 'Progressive redevelopment' in *Official Architecture and Planning*, October.

MORRILL, R. (1965) 'The negro ghetto: problems and alternatives' in *Geographical Review*, 55, pp 339–61.

PEPPER, S. (1971) *Housing improvement: goals and strategies*, Lund Humphries.

STEWART, M. (ed) (1972) *The City: Problems of planning*, Penguin (set book).

STONES, A. (1972) 'Stop slum clearance now' in *Official Architecture and Planning*, February.

STRONG, J. (1885) 'Our country, its possible future and its present crisis' in STRAUSS, A. (ed) (1968) *The American City*, Allen Lane, pp 127–34.

TOWNROE, P. M. (1971) *Industrial Location Decisions*, Occasional Paper 15, Centre for Urban and Regional Studies, University of Birmingham.

WALLACE, D. A. (1968) 'The conceptualizing of urban renewal', *University of Toronto Law Journal*, 18, 3, pp 248–58; reprinted in BOURNE, L. S. (1971), pp 447–55.

WHINSTON, A. B. and DAVIS, O. A. (1961) 'The economics of urban renewal' in *Law and Contemporary Problems*, 26, 1, pp 105–17; reprinted in WILSON, J. (1966) *Urban Renewal*, MIT Press, pp 50–67.

WOLPERT, J. and MUMPHREY, A. (1972) *Metropolitan neighbourhoods: participation and conflict over change*, Commission on College Geography, Association of American Geographers, Resource Paper No 16.

Acknowledgements

Grateful acknowledgement is made to the following sources for material used in this Unit:

Text
American Society of Planning Officials for J. Legler, 'Alternative forms of property taxation as a stimulus to urban redevelopment' in *1971 Planning Yearbook*.

Tables
Centre for Environmental Studies for *Tables 1 and 2* from *The Economics of Urban Residential Renewal and Improvement*, CES Working Paper 77; Controller of Her Majesty's Stationery Office for *Tables 3, 4 and 5*; Notting Hill Peoples Association Housing Group for *Table 6* from *Losing out*; Journal of the American Institute of Planners for *Tables 7 and 8* from C. Hartman, 'The Housing of relocated families' reprinted by permission of the *Journal of the American Institute of Planners*, 30, 4, 1964; George Allen & Unwin Ltd for *Table 9* from J. Cullingworth, *Town and Country Planning in Britain*.

Figures
The City Planning Office, Norwich for *Figures 3, 4 and 8*; Built Environment for *Figure 6* from A. Stones, 'Stop Slum Clearance Now' in *Official Architecture and Planning*, February 1972; Oliver & Boyd for *Figure 7* from P. Jephcott, *Homes in High Flats*.

Plates
Brian Clarke for *Plates 1, 5, 6, 7*.

Unit 29 Planning residential areas
Andrew Blowers

Part cover: Pin Green neighbourhood, Stevenage

Aims
This unit is, in certain respects, related to Unit 7, 'The neighbourhood: exploration of a concept'. You should be familiar with the framework for defining the neighbourhood outlined in that unit.

The overall aim of this unit is to describe and analyse the social planning goals associated with the concept of the neighbourhood unit. This overall aim provides the context for an exploration of three themes which have a far wider significance:

1 The relationship between the social scientist and the planner.

2 The problem of reconciling social planning goals with physical goals.

3 The values implicit in the formulation of both social planning and physical planning goals.

Objectives
After studying this unit you should be able to:

1 Outline the origin and list the main features usually associated with the neighbourhood unit.

2 Describe at least two examples of the application of the neighbourhood unit concept in Britain.

3 Explain the distinction between social and physical planning goals and give examples associated with the neighbourhood unit to illustrate your explanation.

4 Give at least two examples of conflict between social and physical planning goals associated with the neighbourhood unit.

5 Explain the goals of *sense of community* and *social integration* as these terms are used in this unit.

6 Discuss the factors which determine the degree of *sense of community* and *social integration* and describe how far these goals can be measured.

7 Discuss the extent to which these two social goals conflict, and what attempts have been made or could be made to resolve such conflict.

8 Give examples to illustrate the nature of the conflict between the planner and the planned related to the neighbourhood unit.

9 Compare and contrast the social and physical planning goals for the residential areas of Milton Keynes with those of at least one other British new town.

Reading
The unit examines the role of planners in the specific context of residential areas. From this certain conclusions may be drawn which are of general relevance to the goals of planning and the values held by planners. There are five articles in Stewart (1972) which discuss some of the wider issues concerning the relationship of planners to society. They provide a background to the more limited perspective of the unit and one of general relevance to the block as a whole. Two of the articles are required reading and the remaining three are recommended.

The two articles that are *required reading* are:

1 GANS, H. J. (1969) 'Planning for People, not Buildings' in Stewart (1972) pp 363–84.

Gans argues that planners have tended to focus on the physical aspects of planning partly because they believe the environment shapes human behaviour. In fact, social processes, largely ignored by planners, have much more influence on people. Attempts by planners to secure goals such as urbanity or social balance are frequently rejected by people who hold different values. Gans believes that people should, on the whole, be given what they want but where conflicts of interest arise planners should intervene in favour of the poor against the rich.

2 REIN, M. (1969) 'Social Planning: the Search for Legitimacy' in Stewart (1972) pp 425–52.

Rein implicitly assumes that intervention by planners is necessary to achieve social reforms. He explores four sources through which planners can justify their action and he demonstrates the problems that arise in each case. Thus, the planner as *expert* is remote from the political process; as *bureaucrat* he is dependent upon his political masters; as *advocate* he can be the tool of pressure groups; and as *professional* he represents a particular value system. Given the authority to intervene planners employ three alternative strategies of intervention. These are (i) *elite consensus*, by which planners work through existing institutions which tend to impede rather than facilitate reform, (ii) *rational analysis*, which involves using methods of objective scientific enquiry which often fail to perceive important problems or to suggest policies for their solution, (iii) *citizen participation*, which can articulate the needs of the underprivileged but may fail to sustain interest and may provoke conflict among opposing groups.

There is no obvious choice among these alternatives, instead 'a set of intractable problems that are moral in character from which there can be no retreat into technology'.

You will find three questions on these two articles in SAQ 6 at the end of the unit.

The three *recommended articles* are:

1 PAHL, R. E. (1969) 'Whose City' in Stewart (1972) pp 85–91.

Stimulated by Gans' book *People and Plans*, Pahl contemplates the role of the planner in society by comparing the American and British experience. In America 'the progressives want social planning to reduce economic and racial inequality, the conservatives want to defend traditional physical planning and the legitimacy of middle class values' (p 90). In Britain the profession has tended to concentrate on the physical planning goals and to neglect the social ones. Pahl believes all planning is social planning and that planners should concentrate more on the present and less on the future, and focus on the causes rather than the symptoms of urban problems.

2 BUTTIMER, A. (1971) 'Community' in Stewart (1972) pp 195–216.

This is part of a longer article, parts of which are referred to in the unit. The extract given here discusses the nature and approach of community studies. Buttimer identifies the salient social characteristics of working class and middle class suburban areas and she describes the way they can be influenced by planners through housing allocation and layout and design. This article provides a background to those parts of the course where 'community' is a central concept (Block 2, Unit 22, Unit 29 and Unit 33).

3 HARVEY, D. (1971) 'Social Processes, Spatial Form and the Redistribution of Real Income in an Urban System' in Stewart (1972) pp 296–337.

Harvey's main thesis is that existing economic, social and political mechanisms are tending to increase inequalities within the urban environment. He concentrates on the spatial manifestations of inequality. The tendency is for the distribution of external costs and benefits of the location of both public and private facilities to favour the wealthy and powerful rather than the poor and impotent. Intervention to effect a redistribution in favour of the poor is necessary but difficult to specify in terms of conventional economic analysis. He suggests that a hierarchical form of territorial organization offers the most promising framework for resolving conflicts and allocating resources equitably.

1 Introduction
1.1 Planners and social scientists

The planner's[1] function in society is an ambivalent one. Ostensibly he is concerned with the built environment and its adaptation to changing social, economic, and technological demands. In this role he may be seen – and may see himself – as a passive respondent to the changing needs and aspirations of society. But, through his manipulation of the built environment he influences and, in some ways, actively determines aspects of social behaviour. The relationship between man and his built environment is complex, as Unit 6 has shown. Here I shall investigate the role of the planner in that relationship for he is involved in the organization and development of the environment within which people interact. The planning of residential areas will be used to illustrate this theme. More specifically I shall concentrate on the social aspects of planning mainly in new residential areas.

There has been a tendency among planners to confine themselves to the economic and physical aspects of planning. While the social purpose of planning has always been, implicitly, recognized, it has usually been regarded as an aspect of planning that could be identified separately from the economic and physical aspects (see D281, New trends in geography, Unit 12, Part 1, for a critique of this viewpoint; also Gans in Stewart 1972). The social implications of planning have been a subject that social scientists have examined, though in a way often remote from the planning process.[2] Consequently, there has been a tendency to concentrate upon abstract and theoretical issues in planning and to provide empirical data that is difficult to translate into physical planning terms. They 'have not participated in planning as one would expect and when they have it has generally been primarily as critics of assumptions and little more' (Waldorf 1967 p 372). Both planners and sociologists 'have tended to develop self-images and languages which differentiate their approaches to the explanation of problems common to both; each has developed an image and language about the other which has often impeded rather than facilitated mutual understanding' (Buttimer 1971 p 145).[3] Planners have assigned specific tasks to sociologists as gatherers of data by means of social surveys, as investigators of specific social problems, or as evaluators of the outcome of planning projects. Social science, though an essential component, has not been regarded as an integral and inseparable part of the total planning process. There are signs of this situation altering as we shall see, but the transformation is by no means general.

In the past this separation of functions had important consequences. In 1950 Dewey was able to comment that 'the divorce has not only accrued to the disadvantage of the planner, but has lulled the urban sociologist, among other social scientists, into an uncritical complacency' (Dewey 1950 in Hatt and Reiss 1951 p 783). Some social scientists in an effort to apply their work and thereby demonstrate its validity, have provided neat and attractive ideas

---

1 Throughout this unit *planner* and *planning* relate to the profession and process that is responsible for developing the built environment at the local level.

2 Social scientists in this context means those academics, mainly sociologists, who are concerned with the processes that are responsible for the social patterns manifested by society. They may also be interested in the planning implications of their work.

3 A good example of this is the different approach to the spatial patterning of cities. Planners divide cities into zones within which controls on land use are applied (see Unit 14) though this system has become more flexible in Britain with the advent of 'structural' plans to replace land use planning maps. Sociologists have analysed the socio-economic patterns of cities and the ecological processes that have produced them. They have defined, for example, zones in transition where patterns are being transformed. (The article by Burgess in Stewart 1972 provides a classic account of ecological processes in the city.)

suitable for planning experiments. The idea of *social balance* (the integration of people from all socio-economic categories within a defined area) as an alternative to social segregation is an example of this which I shall look at later. Conversely, planners have uncritically accepted some of these ideas as if they were empirically validated theories, and have applied them, often with modifications, to particular planning problems. These mutual misapprehensions may have a profound effect on the built environment and less visibly and measurably upon people's lives as well. The nature and changes in the relationship between social science and planning forms the first main theme of this unit.

1.2 Social goals and physical planning

In Unit 7 I discussed the concept of neighbourhood and reserved consideration of the question 'What are the planning implications of the neighbourhood concept?' for this unit. The problem of reconciling the two dimensions, social and spatial, of neighbourhood was resolved theoretically by the construction of a 'neighbourhood continuum'. In planning terms the reconciliation is by no means simple, partly because some planners have failed to recognize the inherent duality of the concept and have interpreted it as a single dimension (Dewey 1950). They are able to control the tangible aspects of a neighbourhood through a detailed planning brief which provides guidelines for the designers, builders and engineers who must implement their plans. Neighbourhoods may be planned as physical entities but it does not follow that they will develop any social identity as a result.

Neighbourhood, as a sociological concept, implies interaction among people defined as neighbours ('the community neighbourhood', Unit 7). The quality, frequency and selectivity of this interaction will vary according to a range of variables that reflect the demographic and behavioural characteristics of the people and the spatial (design, layout, density) features of the neighbourhood. Individuals will vary, some (especially the less mobile) will be locally orientated while others will belong to interest groups which draw on the urban area as a whole. 'The local type resides in the city but lives in the neighbourhood; the urban type resides in the neighbourhood but lives in the city' (Keller 1968 p 160). Similarly, some people are sociable, while others are reserved, and even apparently homogeneous areas have their subtle social differences such as the 'rough' and 'respectable' types that Kuper noted on working class housing estates (Kuper 1953). The geographical extent of community neighbourhoods differs for each individual, and, when aggregated, they form a series of overlapping personal networks (Unit 7).

As a physical planning concept, neighbourhood consists of the residential area which supports a range of locally based institutions and facilities ('the functional neighbourhood', Unit 7). Among locally based functions are schools, churches and certain shopping, medical and recreational facilities. Except in some very isolated neighbourhoods there is rarely a coincidence between the catchment boundaries of all local functions but rather a set of overlapping functional areas. Neighbourhood planning has tended to centre upon one function – the school – and to relate the provision of other functions to the population and area defined as the school's catchment.

In many cases neighbourhoods for planning purposes are demarcated by reference to natural or man-made boundaries ('the physical neighbourhood', Unit 7), which may or may not have some internal demographic homogeneity ('the homogeneous neighbourhood' Unit 7). Such a compartmentalization of the urban area may impose certain constraints on the location of functions but is not to be confused with planning the neighbourhood according to a set of physical and social principles which is the subject of this unit.

Clearly 'the neighbourhood in planning use is not the same thing as the small groups of people who constitute neighbourhood in the sociological sense' (McConnell 1959 p 83). This point is echoed by Blumenfeld, who asserts that the planning neighbourhood is 'much too large to form social relations that would give content to the title of "neighbourhood" that planners have so confidently bestowed on it' (Blumenfeld 1971 p 178). The planners' approach to the neighbourhood has been concerned, essentially, with the satisfaction of physical planning goals (such as a satisfactory layout within the density constraints, the provision of adequate parking facilities, or the location of service facilities). Social goals have been fitted into this framework. In the case of neighbourhood planning it was found impossible to satisfy both social and physical planning goals through the application of a comprehensive formula based on physical criteria alone. Social goals require a knowledge of social processes if they are to be achieved. The problem of reconciling social and physical goals within a planning framework is the second main theme of this unit.

1.3 Social values and social planning

The values which permeate society (and which influence planners like anyone else) are reflected in various ways in the built environment. Values may influence the location and size of settlements; the design, density, layout and size of residential developments; the location and quality of urban amenities; the balance of public and private housing; the pace and nature of urban renewal (see Unit 28); the role and quality of urban transportation systems and so on. In more specific terms a particular set of values have been responsible for such enduring and visible features of the built environment as new towns, garden suburbs, green belts, high rise flats and pedestrian precincts. Changing values have emphasized one thing rather than another. Hence in the 1950s and early 1960s high rise flats were favoured for inner city redevelopment schemes whereas a reaction against them by the late 1960s was equally pervasive.

The influence of values upon the built environment is not always easy to distinguish. Occasionally, they have been stated as a set of principles that could be translated into physical forms. Such was the case with Ebenezer Howard's 'garden city' concept (1898, 1902), which was expressed in both literary and diagrammatic form (see extract from Howard in Blowers, Hamnett and Sarre (eds) (1974). Also Figure 1, and Audio-visual Handbook 1, Figure 1, p 22). Another example was the 'neighbourhood unit' which gained widespread acclamation and application in the USA, UK and other countries.

The history and influence of the neighbourhood unit idea provide a subject around which to discuss the three underlying themes of this unit:
1 The relationship of social science to planning.
2 The problem of reconciling physical and social planning goals.
3 The significance of values in the planning process.

SAQ 1

In these and subsequent self-assessment questions which are placed at the end of each section you are asked to consider a set of statements. You should examine them critically in terms of their comprehensiveness, relevance and validity. Make notes on each statement on the basis of the correspondence text, the set reading where appropriate, and your own observations. When you have done that compare your comments with those given at the end of the unit.
a   Planners are primarily concerned with the physical environment, social scientists with the social environment.

b The main barrier to mutual understanding between planners and social scientists is a failure to comprehend each other's language.

c Both planners and social scientists recognize the social and spatial components of the neighbourhood concept.

d Planners and social scientists tend to focus on different dimensions of neighbourhood.

2 The neighbourhood unit concept
2.1 Origins of the concept

The neighbourhood unit has diverse origins (Tetlow 1959). In a sense neighbourhoods have always been present in cities beginning, as Mumford (1954) points out, in the various 'quarters' of the medieval city. As a planning concept the neighbourhood unit emanates from different strands of theoretical and practical work undertaken at the turn of the century. On the theoretical side the work of the sociologists Tönnies and Cooley emphasized the significance of the primary community and the natural human tendency for relationships to have a territorial expression in the form of neighbourhoods.

> ... Of the neighbourhood group it may be said, in general, that from the time men formed permanent settlements upon the land, down, at least, to the rise of modern industrial cities, it has played a main part in the primary, heart-to-heart life of the people. (Cooley 1909)

On a more practical level some philanthropists were urging the need for social reforms. In the work of people such as the Barnetts in the East End of London, who advocated social mixing through the educated and privileged living among the poor, the origins of the socially balanced neighbourhood idea may be traced. Their enthusiasm helped to inspire the development of Hampstead Garden Suburb where they hoped people 'of all classes of society, of all sorts of opinion, and all standards of means, can live in helpful neighbourliness' (Barnett 1921). Their utopian ideas were incapable of fulfilment through a physical plan without fundamental changes in the nature of society as well, but they did influence practical planners such as Raymond Unwin the designer of Hampstead Garden Suburb, and later of Letchworth, where he worked with Barry Parker.

The garden city represented another influence on the neighbourhood unit idea. It was the culmination of a number of schemes which, during the nineteenth century, attempted to improve the housing and moral standards of the working

Figure 1 A nineteenth century planned community, Saltaire Source: Yorkshire Evening Post

classes. These schemes had included Saltaire (near Bradford), Bournville (in Birmingham), and Port Sunlight (on Merseyside), each the creation of an industrial patron. But it was Ebenezer Howard who first evolved the principles of design in which the antecedents of the neighbourhood unit are to be found. The ideological nature of his programme is evident in the title of his original book, *Tomorrow: A Peaceful Path to Real Reform* (1898), while the title of the second edition *Garden Cities of Tomorrow* (1902) embodies the infusion of rural values into the urban environment which is a theme of his work. This work has had an impressive influence upon planners for elements of it are to be found in the garden cities and suburbs, green belts, new towns and neighbourhoods built in the first half of the twentieth century.

Howard gives a remarkably precise description of Garden City. Circular in shape and with an optimum population of 32,000 it was to be divided into six identical wards (Figure 2) each triangular in shape with an apex at the city centre, where the civic buildings and a central park are located. Surrounding the park is a crystal palace, a glass covered corridor housing shops and a winter

Figure 2 Howard's Garden City. Layout of one of the six sectoral wards.
Howard's diagrammatic representation of town—country relationships and his concept of a central city linked to satellites are reproduced in Audio-visual Handbook 1, p 22. Source: Howard (1965) p 53

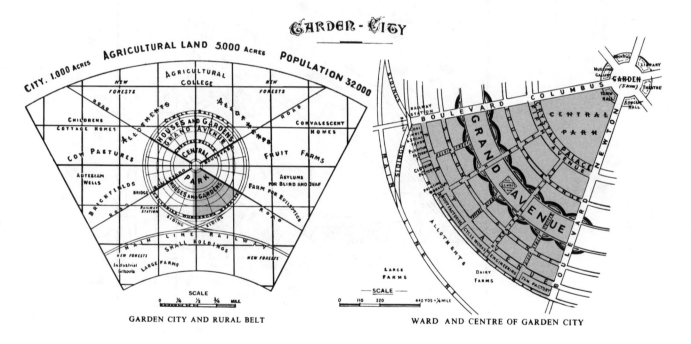

garden. Beyond this is the residential area bisected by a circumferential Grand Avenue providing open space and in which the schools and churches are situated. Industrial sites are confined to the periphery of each ward and served by a circle railway. This plan anticipates some of the important ingredients of the neighbourhood unit – the central open space around the school; the segregation of residential and commercial land uses; the principle of easy access to facilities from all parts of the residential area, while at the same time 'reducing the traffic on the roads of the town', and giving attention to 'varied architecture and design which the houses and groups of houses display'. Although Letchworth and Welwyn Garden City were inspired by Howard's philosophy, in neither case were his proposals fully carried out.

2.2 Clarence Perry's neighbourhood unit scheme

From these various beginnings there emerged some of the distinctive elements of neighbourhood planning theory. The definitive statement of neighbourhood planning principles was made in the 1920s by Clarence Perry (Perry 1929 and 1939). His ideas sprang from his period of residence at Forest Hills Gardens, Long Island, a suburb where 'architectural harmony, its planned community facilities, small interspersed neighbourhood parks, and the specialized character of most of its streets constituted a laboratory for Perry and others thinking along lines of the emerging planned neighbourhood' (Dahir 1947 p 20). He had become aware that most residential areas lack neighbourly life and he attributed this to their anonymity brought about, among other things, by poor location of dwellings, lack of play space, and long journeys to work. His neighbourhood unit formula sought to relate the individual family to a local area in which could be found the facilities needed 'for its comfort and proper development'.

The formula comprised six physical planning principles (Figure 3):

Figure 3 Clarence Perry's neighbourhood unit plan Source: Dahir (1947)

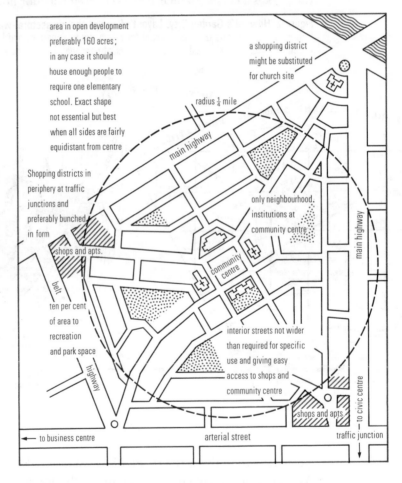

1 School. A centrally located elementary school within a half mile of the furthest dwelling.
The size of the school determines the size of the neighbourhood which, in practice, could vary between 3,000 and 10,000 people. The population density would vary according to location, though even in low density suburban neighbourhoods, a smaller school size would ensure that the half-mile radius was not exceeded.

2 Boundaries. These should be formed by the major roads so that no through traffic should enter the neighbourhood.

3 Open space. Within each neighbourhood ten per cent of the area should be devoted to open space including playing fields, small parks and small areas scattered throughout.

4 Institutional buildings. At the centre of the unit the community buildings – school, library, club, church – would be grouped around a square.

5 Retail districts. Neighbourhood shopping centres should be located on the periphery of each unit at junctions of boundary roads so that part of each of three units could be served from each centre.

6 Internal street layout. Roads serving the neighbourhood should be of varying width and designed to accommodate intra neighbourhood traffic effectively. The layout and architectural design would, together, create a harmonious residential environment.

Perry considered his scheme to be applicable to redevelopment areas as well as to new developments. Wherever it was applied it would, in his view, nurture face-to-face relationships which he considered to be 'a normal feature of the environment of society'.[1] It is fair to point out, however, that Perry did not import into his scheme the goals of social balance and community spirit that have come to be associated with it. Although he was 'concerned with the social aspects of his plan, they did not form the basis for it. His assumption that close, intimate relationships would develop was just that, an assumption' (Waldorf 1967 p 373).

2.3 The diffusion of the neighbourhood unit scheme

The neighbourhood unit scheme diffused slowly at first and was largely confined to the USA in the interwar years. Clarence Stein and Henry Wright in the 1920s (before Perry's ideas had been publicly formulated) built Sunnyside, Long Island and more importantly, Radburn, New Jersey, with layouts especially designed to segregate pedestrians from traffic and to stimulate social interaction (Figure 4). Radburn layouts, with car parking at the rear of dwellings and

Figure 4a The Radburn plan This is a diagrammatic representation of the classic Radburn layout. The neighbourhood is in the form of a 'superblock' defined by a ring road. At the centre is a primary school and fingers of open space penetrating the residential areas. These are reached by short roads which provide traffic with rear entry to homes, leaving the fronts free for pedestrian access. Source: L. Keeble (1969) *Principles and Practice of Town and Country Planning*

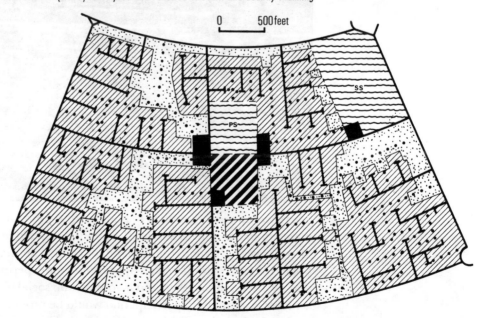

---

[1] This is, of course, a value judgement on Perry's part, for some people, notably cosmopolitans (Unit 8), face-to-face relationships within the locality are relatively unimportant.

Figure 4b The plates illustrate the rear access and garaging (left) to the houses which face a walkway (right)

pedestrian walkways at the front, were subsequently incorporated into many neighbourhood schemes both in the USA and Britain.

The neighbourhood unit plan itself tended to be introduced in scattered private developments in the USA (Dahir 1947). In Britain it became associated mainly with public housing schemes. The large Wythenshawe estate in Manchester built during the interwar years was planned according to neighbourhood unit principles but, like the even larger contemporary Becontree estate at Dagenham (Figure 5) it was essentially a one-class suburb. In the postwar boom of housing construction the neighbourhood unit scheme was virtually axiomatic in large public housing developments.

Figure 5 Becontree estate, Dagenham   Photo: Aerofilms Ltd.

There were a combination of reasons for this. First, there was a reaction among planners and architects against the undifferentiated urban sprawl of the interwar years. Second, the demand for council housing immediately after the Second World War offered an opportunity for experiment. Thirdly, it was felt that by attention to design and layout certain social objectives could be achieved. Community participation would be promoted by social balance and by the physical plan of the neighbourhood. This belief in the social determinism of physical planning rested largely on the unproven assertions and uncontested assumptions of the conventional planning wisdom of the time.

Neighbourhood unit planning was given official endorsement by the Dudley Report (1944) which set guidelines on the size, density, layout and amenities of residential areas. A 'target' population of 10,000 was recommended dependent on two schools for the 5–11 year age group, and of 5,000 where there was only one such school. Each neighbourhood would be 'self-contained' providing in addition to schools a number of local services such as churches, a library, a public house, a clinic, and shops at the neighbourhood 'centre'. Monotony in the layout would be avoided through a varied street pattern and open spaces would be scattered throughout and around the periphery to act as a buffer between neighbourhoods. These design principles were largely adopted in postwar neighbourhoods. Certain sociological notions which make their appearance in the Dudley Report also had an important bearing on subsequent planning attitudes. It was argued that a 'sense of neighbourhood' would be achieved in a unit that was 'large enough (i) to embrace a wide variety of experience and tastes, and yet small enough (ii) to possess easy accessibility between its parts, and (iii) to provide occasion for acquaintance' (Dudley Report 1944 p 59). The Report also suggested that social balance could be achieved through neighbourhood planning. In doing so it revealed a widely held value judgement.

... A great deal of evidence has been submitted indicating that each neighbourhood should be 'socially balanced', inhabited by families belonging to different ranges of income groups, or at least not so unbalanced as to be restricted to dwellings and families of one type or income only, as the case may be. (Dudley Report 1944 p 61)

The evidence is nowhere quoted and little indication is given of how these social goals are to be achieved beyond a discussion of site planning.

... The way to success would lie ... in so arranging the dwellings within the neighbourhood plan that it is made up of several minor groups of dwellings, each one of which would have its own distinctive character. (Dudley Report 1944 p 61)

Application of these principles was encouraged in three influential planning documents produced during and just after the Second World War in the *County of London Plan* (1943), *The Greater London Plan* (1944), and *The New Towns Commission Final Report* (1946). The London plans emphasize the need for physically defined neighbourhood units which would inculcate a sense of community, and be a 'means of resolving what would otherwise be interminable aggregations of housing'. The form of their proposed neighbourhoods follows very closely the recommendation of the Dudley Report. The New Towns Commission adopted neighbourhood units enthusiastically as an essential element in the creation of new communities.

Backed by new legislation (the New Towns Act, 1946, and The Town and Country Planning Act, 1947) planners were able to implement the neighbourhood plan in various public housing schemes throughout the country. In the London area, inner area redevelopment schemes such as Stepney–Poplar were based upon it. At the same time the ring of interwar out-county estates (Becontree, Watling, St Helier, etc) was encircled by an outer ring of thirteen estates (Figure 6) forming urbanized enclaves within the newly defined Green Belt (Figure 7): see Blowers (1973). These varied in size from Hutton (485 dwellings, 1,600 population) to Harold Hill (7,600 dwellings, 29,000 population). Despite variations in size the LCC considered the neighbourhood plan appropriate to each. 'That much of this work is based on the concept of neighbourhood planning requires no elaboration' (London County Council 1949). These redevelopment and overspill housing schemes were complemented

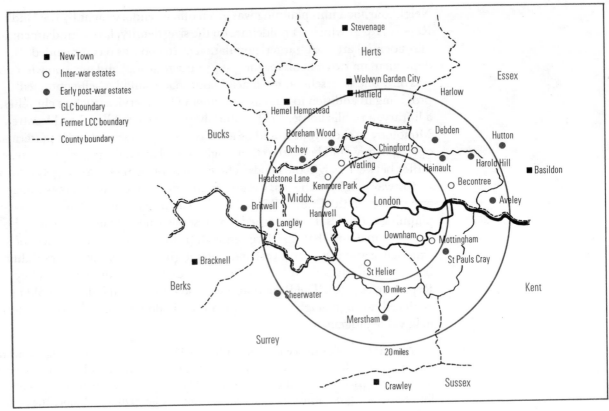

Figure 6 Out-county estates and new towns in the London region

by the creation of new towns and the expansion of existing ones. Eight of the new towns formed a ring around London beyond the Green Belt (Figure 6) and in each of them the neighbourhood unit principle was applied. Although the size of units varied widely both within and between the new towns (Osborn and Whittick 1963) in each considerable effort was made to give them physical identity and in some, for example Stevenage and Crawley, neighbourhood names and colours were added to signposts and street names (Figure 8). This, incidentally, seems to have had little effect on individual perceptions of neighbourhood, for in Stevenage Willmott (1962) found that less than a third of those he interviewed knew the name of the neighbourhood in which they lived.

The neighbourhood plan as it was applied in those postwar years differed somewhat from Perry's model (Goss 1961). Instead of a social centre with a

Figure 7 Debden estate, near Loughton, Essex

Stevenage

Figure 8 Identification of neighbourhood units in Stevenage

The town is divided into clearly demarcated neighbourhoods (a). Each is clearly indicated on the directional signs by name and a specific colour (b) and (c). The colour is used on all signs in each neighbourhood (d). Residential areas are segregated from traffic (e) and pathways connect the houses to the local shopping centre (f).

school, community buildings and open space, these neighbourhoods had a commercial emphasis with much of the open space on the outskirts (Figure 9). Since many of them were urban fringe or new town neighbourhoods densities were comparatively low. The application of neighbourhood planning was fairly

flexible and in Harlow new town 'clusters' of neighbourhood units were designed around district shopping centres giving the hierarchical expression to the plan that has re-emerged in more recent new town schemes.

By the early 1950s the neighbourhood plan had achieved widespread acceptance. Collison (1954) discovered that four-fifths of the planning authorities in England and Wales employed the concept to some extent and that a third of the county borough authorities[1] adopted it in every development scheme. In county authorities, settlements were often too small or contained too many existing structures for the principles to be applied in redevelopment schemes. Collison concluded that although planners at that time accepted the theory as a basis for 'solving traffic problems and integrating amenities with housing' they were less impressed by the social advantages the plan was alleged to confer on residential areas. For example a town planning report for Bedford published at this time (1952) says:

... A medium sized town, in particular, can be seen more easily as a social unit than any of its separate neighbourhoods ... yet, at the same time the physical barrier of the rivers and the railways, and the social contrast between the districts, have given rise to fairly well defined neighbourhood units. (Lock, Grove and King 1952 p 93)

There were signs in the early 1950s of increasing disenchantment with the neighbourhood unit concept. In particular the incompatibility of certain social and political goals within a rigid physical planning framework was widely recognized. This reaction drew attention to the need for greater understanding of social processes and the necessity for the inherent values in the planning process to be consistent with the planning outcome. The themes we identified

1 County Boroughs, abolished as a result of local government reorganization, represent the largest urban authorities.

earlier (see Section 1.3) had become the focus of the debate which surrounded the neighbourhood planning concept. Moreover, this was a debate which could begin to draw upon the empirical evidence supplied by numerous planning experiments. The debate is intrinsically interesting but also has wider implications for the relationship of planners to society.

SAQ 2 Comment critically on the following statements and then refer to the comments at the end of the unit.

a The idea of the socially balanced neighbourhood originated as the means for achieving social reform.

b In his neighbourhood unit scheme Clarence Perry aimed to secure social goals through physical planning.

c The emphasis on social goals in Perry's scheme was a major reason for its widespread acceptance.

d In Britain neighbourhood planning was based upon a set of planning principles rather than a detailed physical plan.

3 The social goals of neighbourhood planning
3.1 The major social goals

In social terms the major assumptions of the early neighbourhood plans were that a *sense of community* (or sense of neighbourhood in the words of the Dudley Report) and *social integration* were desirable and that they could be fostered by physical planning. These assumptions reflected the hope, which in some cases was a belief, that the neighbourhood unit offered a panacea for the social problems attributable to urbanization. 'Neighbourhood unit organization seems the practical answer to the giantism and inefficiency of the over-centralized metropolis' (Mumford 1954). The major social goals, then, were a sense of community and social integration. They were to be achieved through the neighbourhood plan. The planning implications for each are different and for this reason they will be treated separately.

3.2 The goal of community

'A good community is easier to recognize than define' (PEP 1949). The problem of defining what constitutes a community has been discussed extensively elsewhere (Bell and Newby 1972; Blowers in D281, Unit 11, Part 2). The concept includes a number of elements and may be broadly summarized as a feeling of belonging to a particular territorial or social group within which there is a sense of identity and a high level of social interaction. In these terms a neighbourhood (but not necessarily a neighbourhood unit) may form a community, as Unit 7 showed.

The community neighbourhood is a far cry from the extravagant claims made by some protagonists of the neighbourhood unit plan. These were summarized by L. E. White as a belief that 'our modern urban civilization can best be rebuilt by recovering all that is worthwhile in the small "primary" group with its face-to-face contacts as typified in the village tradition' (White 1950). The urban neighbourhood in no way replicates the traditional pre-industrial village. In a village individuals are known to each other in a variety of private and public roles. 'The overlapping of numerous economic as well as social relations within a limited geographical area gives to even the most superficial of social contacts economic significance' (Riemer 1951). Individual social networks are close knit and largely confined to the village, and in consequence social control is easily exercised over all the inhabitants. In the city people tend to work outside their neighbourhood however it may be defined. Most people, except the least mobile, have social networks that extend beyond the boundaries of their neighbourhood. Individual social networks may involve people in particular role relationships in a community of interest that is spatially dispersed or with one that is confined to a specific and contiguous area.

An analysis of these role relationships provides a measure of social interaction and hence an indication of the social content of the notion of 'sense of community'. There are two types of relationships within the neighbourhood community which may be used in this way. These are participation in voluntary and formal associations and patterns of neighbour and friendship formation.

3.2.1 Voluntary and formal association

Formal or voluntary associations may be defined as bodies whose 'functions are characterized by explicit regularity and standardization' (Axelrod 1956) and they include all except commercial concerns, government departments and schools. The level of participation in these associations is related to the status of neighbourhoods. Axelrod found a high level of participation (sixty-three per cent belonging to an association) among a Detroit sample population but one that varied directly and positively with income, occupational status and education. Bell and Force (1956) comparing neighbourhoods in San Francisco discovered that in high status neighbourhoods adult males belonged to more associations (Table 1), attended them more frequently and were more likely to hold office in them than in low status neighbourhoods. When individual economic status was held constant they found that men living in high status neighbourhoods tended to participate more than those in low status ones. This they considered was a result either of the individual's self-image not conforming to his objectively measured social status, or of group pressures being applied in order to achieve conformity to group norms.

Table 1   Percentage of men having membership in a certain number of formal associations

Number of groups	Low family Low economic (Mission) %	Low family High economic (Pacific Heights) %	High family Low economic (Outer Mission) %	High family High economic (St Francis Wood) %
7 or more	1.7	11.0	0	19.0
6	0	2.6	0	4.2
5	1.2	3.2	1.2	11.9
4	2.3	7.3	2.9	13.7
3	11.6	11.5	8.8	17.3
2	22.1	23.0	22.4	13.7
1	37.8	19.9	44.7	13.1
None	23.3	21.5	19.4	7.1
Not ascertained	0	0	0.6	0

The table shows how, in a sample of males in San Francisco, participation in formal associations (indicated by, measured by membership) was greatest in the neighbourhoods of highest economic status (ie Pacific Heights, St Francis Wood). It was highest where high economic status and family status were combined (St Francis Wood).

Source: Bell and Force (1956) Table 2

Given that participation in formal associations appears to be quite high but varies according to the status of neighbourhood, what functions do such associations perform? Do they provide a means whereby individuals may *integrate* themselves into a neighbourhood and thereby enjoy primary, personal, and informal association or do they act as a *substitute* for such relationships reflecting the anonymity and impersonality that is the characteristic of urban society according to some writers? Litwak (1961) concluded from the available evidence, that, despite the importance of national institutions local identification was still important; that increasing geographical and social mobility did not necessarily preclude local commitment; and that voluntary association was an important means by which neighbourhood cohesion was achieved. His own research in Buffalo suggested a cycle of neighbourhood cohesion for individual families. This cohesion describes families that have a positive neighbourhood

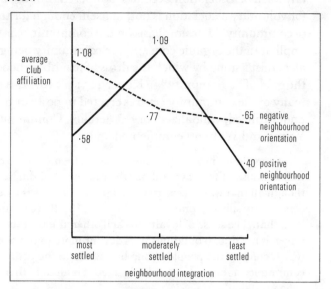

Figure 10 Neighbourhood orientation by average club association The figures represent the average number of clubs to which individuals in each of these categories belonged. The curvilinear relationship of those with a positive neighbourhood orientation can be compared with the linear relationship of those with a negative neighbourhood orientation. The figures are based on a sample from Buffalo, USA. Source: Litwak (1961)

orientation, ie those who wish to develop personal relationships within the neighbourhood. The cycle has three stages (Figure 10). Stage 1 is the settling in period during which the family is home centred in its efforts to adjust to residential change and possibly, a new occupation. During the second stage families are likely to participate fairly intensively in formal associations in an effort to establish more intimate personal relationships in their neighbourhood. The third stage represents the settled family where primary relationships are firmly established and participation in formal association tends to be more selective. Families who follow this cycle therefore have statistically speaking an asymmetrical curvilinear relationship between neighbourhood integration and participation in formal associations (Figure 10). In such cases formal associations perform an integrative function. For those families who do not have a positive neighbourhood orientation (ie do not wish to form personal relationships within the neighbourhood) the curve is linear indicating that participation in formal associations over time and substitutes for more informal relationships.

Litwak found the curvilinear integrative relationship (ie the inverted V-shape of Figure 10) typical of all classes except the upwardly mobile who had a more negative attitude towards neighbourhood cohesion.

These studies have tended to concentrate on the socio-economic variables that determine the level of participation in voluntary associations. They indicate the differences that occur between and within neighbourhoods and reveal some of the processes involved in the development of the neighbourhood community. The role of voluntary associations in community formation is a mediatorial one. Axelrod suggests that 'insofar as such organizations exercise any pervasive influence in the urban community, it may be through links between the minority of active members and the underlying network of informal association in the community at large'. The inference is that the informal association among friends and neighbours is more important in promoting neighbourhood cohesion. All this adds up to little guidance to the planner. Even if the spatial aspects of formal associations were dealt with more adequately there remains the doubt whether the promotion of such association would stimulate community development leaving aside the question of whether this is desirable in any case. From the evidence it would seem that physical factors have very little to do with voluntary participation.

Obviously where no community facilities are provided the establishment of any form of association becomes hampered. But the mere provision of facilities for voluntary association is not, in itself, enough for the development of a sense of community. 'The emphasis on the community centre is linked with the values implicit in the organic concept, the community being conceived as a sort of alchemist's stone by which the dross of neighbourhood may be transformed into the gold of "community" ' (Kuper 1951 p 239). It is not surprising that so many of the community centres erected in postwar neighbourhoods were underutilized, vandalized, or left derelict. Community is not so easily created. Young and Willmott commented on this:

... even where the town planners have set themselves to create communities anew as well as houses, they have still put their faith in buildings, sometimes speaking as though all that was necessary for neighbourliness was a neighbourhood unit, for community spirit a community centre ... But there is surely more to a community than that. The sense of loyalty to each other amongst the inhabitants of Bethnal Green is not due to buildings. It is due far more to ties of kinship and friendship which connect the people of one household to the people of another. In such a district community does not have to be fostered it is already there. (Young and Willmott 1962 pp 198–9)

They emphasize the significance of primary relationships in community formation. This is a second way of measuring neighbourhood cohesion.

3.2.2 Informal social relations

Several studies have emphasized the importance of primary relationships in the formation of the neighbourhood community. It is important to distinguish between the types of informal relationship that may exist, of which interaction with neighbours is only one. Axelrod found in his study that, in terms of frequency of association, relatives were far more important than neighbours, and that visits among friends tended to be more frequent than among neighbours. Only work colleagues were less important as a group with whom visits were exchanged. Visiting is only one indicator but it suggests a degree of intimacy and underlines the qualitative differences in social interaction.[1] Bell and Boat (1957) working on the San Francisco data mentioned earlier also found that 'kin are more likely to provide intimate social contacts than neighbours or co-workers in each neighbourhood'. They related the frequency and intimacy of informal contacts among adult males to the major indices of economic and family status.[2] In those areas with high family status (many children, a low proportion of women in the labour force, and many single-family detached dwellings) informal participation was greatest. Social isolation (cases where individual participation occurs only once a year or less) was highest in the neighbourhood of low family and low economic status. Here fifty-seven per cent of the men were isolated from their neighbours and even in the high family and high economic status neighbourhoods about a third were isolated from neighbours. This kind of study, though limited in scope and confined to male adults (we should expect quite different findings for females) does bring

[1] In a neighbourhood like Bethnal Green considerable interaction takes place on the doorstep and in the street (see part cover and plates 8d and f of Unit 7). Visiting is, perhaps, more a feature of middle class than working class relationships (Unit 7).
[2] These indices derive from two of the constructs of social area analysis (Shevky and Bell 1955). There are three constructs each representing changes in the social structure as the scale of society grows through industrialization. They are social rank (economic status), urbanization (family status) and segregation (ethnic status). Social area analysis is fully explained in D281 Block III Unit 10.

out two important points: 1 that people depend upon kin and friends rather than upon neighbours, and 2 that social participation is greatest in areas of high family status. These are both relevant to planning:

1 Community is a complex social system and can be disrupted or destroyed by planning intervention. If the maintenance or development of a sense of community is valued then the alternative planning strategies are clear. Either existing communities should be preserved and a policy of physical revitalization pursued or, where this proves impossible in areas where housing is outworn, disruption of the community should be minimized by giving people, especially kin, the opportunity to move together to a new development rather than dispersing them. This is, however, a question of housing management and allocation rather than one of physical planning.

2 The level of participation will depend largely on the characteristics of people in individual neighbourhoods. To some extent this, too, can be influenced by housing allocation policies. For instance families at a certain stage in the life cycle and of similar socio-economic status can be concentrated together in public housing schemes or attracted towards certain types of housing in private schemes. The design and layout of estates may influence the initiation of contacts and act as a catalyst in community development. But housing management and environmental design are not all that is required to generate community spirit, indeed they may not in every case be necessary.

3.3 The goal of social integration
3.3.1 Racial and socio-economic integration

The goal of social integration implies that a population representative of all age groups and socio-economic classes lives within the same area. It therefore tends to conflict with the goal of sense of community which is best attained through some form of social segregation. At its most radical, the goal of social integration aimed at changing the prevailing social structure by influencing the spatial structure of society. It was based on the belief that the spatial structure was a cause rather than an effect of the social structure. The means of achieving this was to be the 'socially balanced' neighbourhood unit. The emphasis varied. In Britain it was seen as a way of overcoming class barriers, in America those of race. Both social and economic advantages would accrue from integration. On the social side the presence of a variety of age groups, attitudes and interests in a neighbourhood would lead to broader horizons and mutual toleration. At an economic level gross inequalities which are emphasized by segregation might gradually be reduced. How this would be achieved was not made clear. Integration in itself would have no effect on private income distribution though it might have an effect on the distribution of public services. It might, for example, reduce the educational differences that occur between affluent and deprived neighbourhoods.[1] This might have profound social consequences. These arguments were attractive but contained a mixture of social realism and wishful thinking. 'Despite a continuing ideological predilection for "social balance", and "integration" there is considerable empirical evidence on the wishes of people to live with people of their own class' (Buttimer in Stewart 1972 p 205). Integration might also provoke discord and exacerbate latent conflicts. The social structure is too complex for a universally applicable solution to social problems.

In some circumstances social integration through the neighbourhood unit might help overcome the exclusiveness of caste or class, if not of income. In the USA housing segregation is reinforced by zoning laws and special covenants on

1 In the absence of integration the authorities might, as in the UK, discriminate positively in favour of deprived areas.

housing developments (see Unit 9, especially Section 8). Deutsch and Collins (1955) compared an integrated (negro and white) housing project with a segregated one in New Jersey. The housing was for low income groups so that differences of economic status between the two groups were absent. They argued since the housing was at the lower end of the housing market it was unlikely that people would deliberately seek to live there, so the problem of self-selection was also effectively eliminated from the study. Further, the researchers were also able to control other intervening variables such as political attitudes, prejudice, and previous experience of integration. Their results indicated that in integrated housing areas the races held much more favourable attitudes towards each other than in non-integrated areas. Other studies (eg Merton 1951) have confirmed more positive attitudes when integration takes place. However, when racial prejudice is ingrained as in the USA's Deep South, where races differ in economic status, or where there is economic competition between them, conflict is more likely. Desegregation is only one means of achieving racial tolerance. Education and changes in the economic structure are others. Once again, a deeper understanding of the social process at work is necessary before the results of a scheme of planned integration can be predicted.

In Britain social segregation in the private housing sector has been maintained by a variety of means. These include 'economic and financial selection due to inability to purchase or rent homes in exclusive areas, outright refusal to lease or sell to "undesirables", social ostracism of unwanted newcomers by old timers, and, as a desperate last gesture, the abandonment of the area by old residents . . .' (Keller 1966). In the public sector the principle of subsidized housing for families with low incomes or who suffer overcrowding or other deprivations, and who can satisfy the residential requirements has effectively restricted the scope for social integration. In some schemes, however, there has been an admixture of council and private housing in an effort to achieve social balance. The New Towns Commission were forthright on this subject:

. . . So far as the issue is an economic one, balance can be attained by giving opportunity for many sorts of employment which will attract men and women up to a high income level. Beyond that point the problem is not economic at all, nor even a vaguely social one; it is to be frank, one of class distinction . . . if the community is to be truly balanced, so long as social classes exist, all must be represented in it. (New Towns Commission 1946)

In the early new towns an attempt was made to apply the principle, for example in Crawley the planners aimed to achieve a similar balance to that of England and Wales in the local population within each neighbourhood. According to

Table 2 Class structures of new towns, with comparisons

Social Class	Crawley 1961	Harlow 1957	Hemel Hempstead 1960	England and Wales 1961	Greater London 1961	Dagenham 1958
I Professional	3.7%	5.0%	5.9%	3.8%	4.8%	1%
II Intermediate Professional	13.4%	13.0%	20.1%	15.4%	15.8%	4%
III Unskilled non-manual and skilled manual	63.6%	63.0%	54.6%	51.1%	52.2%	56%
IV Semi-skilled manual	13.1% }	19.0%	14.4%	20.5%	18.1%	22%
V Unskilled manual	6.2% }		5.0%	9.2%	9.1%	17%
Middle Class (Classes I & II)	17.1%	18.0%	26.0%	19.2%	20.6%	5%
Working Class (Classes III, IV and V)	82.9%	82.0%	74.0%	80.8%	79.4%	95%

Source: Heraud (1968) Table 1

Heraud (1968) this was largely achieved taking the population over the town as a whole (though Crawley had a relatively high proportion of manual workers). By comparison with Dagenham, the interwar working class estate, the balance attained in Crawley was striking (Table 2). Within the town segregation has occurred as a result of three factors:

1 the initial population influx was largely working class and occupied the first neighbourhoods to be established near the town centre.

2 the later arrival of service and professional workers combined with a policy of building executive houses on the outskirts led to the outer ring of neighbourhoods having a high proportion of middle class residents.

3 social segregation has increased as a result of intra-urban migration since the town was established. The degree of segregation in Crawley is described by the indices of dissimilarity and segregation shown in Table 3. In Crawley, as in other new towns, there was never any attempt at integration within every group of houses. Instead a compromise was attempted in the form of neighbourhood balance but with internal segregation in housing clusters within it.

Table 3 Indices of dissimilarity and segregation, Crawley 1961

Social Class	1	2	Dissimilarity 3	4	5	Segregation
I Professional occupation		18	16	32	25	17
II Intermediate professional			16	33	10	17
III Skilled manual and unskilled non-manual				22	15	6
IV Semi-skilled manual occupation					27	22
V Unskilled manual occupations						13

Source: Heraud (1968) Table 7

The main arguments in favour of a policy of small-scale segregation within an integrated neighbourhood is that it minimizes conflict and facilitates interaction within homogeneous housing clusters while providing opportunity for social integration within the heterogeneous neighbourhood. There is little evidence to support the latter argument, rather the reverse. Differentiation of housing types within a neighbourhood adds physical identity to social boundaries and inhibits interaction.

3.3.2 Integration of age groups

Social integration is not only a question of reducing class barriers, for differences in age are also important. For the young and old, the least mobile groups, the neighbourhood is likely to be the locus of satisfaction of most economic and social needs. The old are an especially vulnerable group who, on retirement, lose their status and become increasingly dependent upon relatives, friends and neighbours, and the statutory and voluntary social services. Living alone they may suffer from social isolation. The question as to whether it is desirable for old people to be concentrated together or whether they should be dispersed is not easy to answer in absolute terms. The little available evidence suggests that the old should be able to live near people of their own age groups within an area containing people of all ages.

Rosow (1967) studied the friendship patterns of old people in neighbourhoods in Cleveland, Ohio. He found that where old people were concentrated they were able to make more friendships than in those situations where old people formed a small proportion of the population. He concluded that 'since the aged suffer from lower status in the larger society in several respects, placing them in the position of neighbours with young people would inhibit the development of friendship'.

The implication here is that housing allocation and development policies should afford some concentration of old people. However, this does not mean that they should be segregated into retirement colonies. Evidence from my own researches indicates that old people wish to be near their children and grandchildren but not necessarily to live with them. On the North Kenton estate, Newcastle upon Tyne (mentioned in Unit 7) there was a marked contrast between those old people living in clusters of self-contained bungalows (Figure 11) scattered throughout the estate and those living in flats which formed the ground floor of maisonette or flat blocks (Figures 12 and 13) containing young families (Blowers 1970). The former expressed considerable satisfaction with their housing environment, the latter generally liked their dwelling but not its

Figure 11 North Kenton estate, Newcastle-upon-Tyne   A group of self-contained old persons' dwellings.   Source: Ashley Selby

Figure 12 North Kenton estate, Newcastle-upon-Tyne   Three storey maisonettes. The maisonettes occupy the two upper floors, and the old persons' flats are on the ground floor.   Source: Ashley Selby

Figure 13 North Kenton estate, Newcastle-upon-Tyne   Five storey point blocks. Point blocks have a cruciform plan. Each block has eight maisonettes (two per wing) with four old persons' flats occupying the ground floor. There is a single entrance and central stairway to the blocks.   Source: Ashley Selby

Figure 14 North Kenton estate, Newcastle-upon-Tyne   Example of vandalism on the estate.   Source: Ashley Selby

situation. They suffered from noise created by families above them, and, in the case of the point-blocks (Figure 13), on all four sides as well. Such a conflict of interests between old people who want peace and young children who need play space is a common one and stems from a failure to recognize the social aspects of housing and estate design. Although design is unlikely to erase all the problems, for the satisfaction of old people also depends on the proximity of kin, it helps to avoid conflict.

Another group likely to suffer isolation are adolescents. The depredations young people wreak on housing estates is frequently attributed to a lack of facilities for them. While this may be a contributory factor it is hardly likely to be chiefly responsible since well-provided estates are often as vandalized (Figure 14) as those entirely lacking in facilities. Part of the explanation may lie in the type of provision made for young people. Institutionalized youth clubs represent the paternalistic social control that adults seek to exercise over adolescents. What is required are more spontaneous means for self-expression such as discotheques. Another part of the explanation may lie in the ambiguous status of adolescents and a lack of a clearly defined set of expectations for them. At a more psychological level Rosenberg (1965) studied adolescent self-images in New York State and found that those belonging to minority groups (religious in this case) tended to suffer from lower self-esteem. In a British context minority groups, apart from ethnic ones, are not so sharply defined. Rosenberg's study suggests, at a wider level, that a feeling of group solidarity is necessary for self-esteem and therefore a policy of desegregation must avoid the creation of social isolation among members of the minority group. Rosenberg puts it this way:

... As long as the mixture is fairly even, benefits will accrue to both groups – for the majority an opportunity to discard false prejudices; for the minority sufficient support from group identification to fend off rejection by the majority, and to project a positive self-image onto the minority. (Rosenberg 1965)

3.4 Summary of social goals

The major social goals of neighbourhood planning (the development of community, and social integration) though obviously related imply different planning outcomes. This problem is illustrated diagrammatically in Figure 15.

Figure 15 Social goals and planning outcomes Source: Andrew Blowers

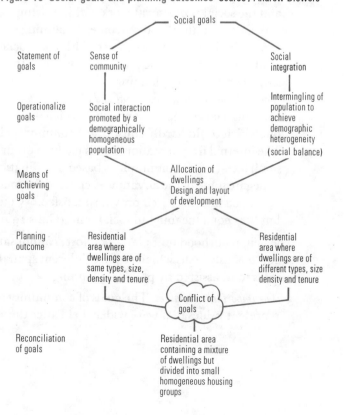

The development of a sense of community requires some segregation in order that interaction is encouraged among demographically homogeneous and socially compatible neighbours. Conversely, social integration demands the formation of heterogeneous neighbourhoods. There are two means by which planners can influence the achievement of these social goals:

1 The most important is by controlling or seeking to influence the population structure through the housing allocation mechanism or through the development of a particular dwelling mix and density designed to attract people of the same or different incomes and family size. The degree of influence the planner himself can exert will vary widely and depend upon the relative powers of other agents involved in the allocation of land and dwellings.

2 The planner has more control over the design of a neighbourhood and can exert some influence on its social development. As was demonstrated in Units 6 and 7, functional distances and the location of facilities can have an important bearing on the initiation if not the maintenance of social contacts.

The goal of community requires either the allocation of dwellings to specific social groups or the development of housing types designed to attract a socially (and economically) homogeneous population. Social integration uses the same mechanism to obtain the opposite result. It is, theoretically, possible to accommodate both goals within the same planning framework. This involves establishing macro-neighbourhoods (equivalent in scale to those of the neighbourhood unit plan) containing a heterogeneous population divided into micro-neighbourhoods each with a homogeneous population. In this way there will be, according to Gans (1961), sufficient homogeneity to prevent severe stress or conflict, and enough heterogeneity to prevent serious inequalities. Such a framework sets broad planning parameters.

It is, however, clear that planning alone cannot dictate social relationships and that a simple but rigid formula is incapable of global application. At this stage it is worth considering the question of social goals in terms of the three major themes elicited in Section 1:

1 *The problem of communication between planners and social scientists.* It is obvious from the sociological research that social goals are difficult to formulate and to operationalize. Much more needs to be known about residents' desires and the social processes at work within existing communities before predictions on the social outcome of planning strategies for new communities can be made with any assurance. Although social scientists have often been unable to define specific planning objectives their work does highlight the social constraints of planning.

2 *The problem of reconciling social and physical goals.* The neighbourhood unit contains a large population within which social balance could be achieved but which could hardly constitute a community in the sense I have used it. The internal fragmentation that is likely to occur with the development of small face-to-face communities based on affiliation to status groups is likely to negate some of the advantages claimed for social integration. The neighbourhood unit may well provide a satisfactory functional planning entity but 'it is not a meaningful social unit' (Gans 1961).

The neighbourhood unit plan, therefore, cannot satisfy logically and simultaneously goals which require different spatial outcomes if their achievement is to be assisted by physical planning.

3 *The importance of values.* The goals of community and social integration represent values that were widely held after the Second World War and the

latter remains an important egalitarian principle. The tendency is for planners' values to derive from a middle class, liberal viewpoint leaving them open to the criticism that these values may not coincide with those of the inhabitants of their planned neighbourhoods. This may be a contributory factor in the way planned communities are used. For example, community centres may be ignored, playspace misused, gardens neglected, or amenities disfigured. The failure of postwar neighbourhood planning to attain the goals of its most ardent enthusiasts underlines a familiar but fundamental issue – that values are difficult to impose on those unwilling to accept them. Consent is necessary for success and planning policies if they are to succeed must be regarded as the effects of and not the cause of social changes.

SAQ 3 Comment on these statements and then refer to the comments given at the end of the unit.

a Advocates of the neighbourhood unit idea hoped that it would foster the creation of neighbourhood communities.

b Participation in voluntary or formal associations provides a good measure of the sense of community in neighbourhoods.

c Interaction among neighbours provides a good measure of the sense of community in neighbourhoods.

d The sense of community in a neighbourhood depends very largely on the shared characteristics of its inhabitants.

e The socially balanced neighbourhood is a means of reducing social and economic inequalities.

f The goals of sense of community and social integration cannot be achieved simultaneously in the context of the neighbourhood unit plan.

g The goals of sense of community and social integration in the neighbourhood can be achieved through the allocation of housing.

4 Recent approaches to residential area planning in Britain

By the middle of the 1950s the neighbourhood unit plan had attracted considerable opprobrium both from sociologists who doubted its social assumptions (Kuper 1951, Dennis 1958, Mann 1958) and from planners who recognized the rigidity it imposed upon their planning. This disillusionment led, predictably, to a reaction against the neighbourhood unit and its rejection by many planners as an acceptable basis for residential planning. This culminated in the designs for the so-called Mark 2 new towns[1] of Cumbernauld constructed outside Glasgow and Hook proposed for Hampshire but never built. Both were conceived in the late 1950s on the principle of a high density continuous built up area the majority of which was within easy walking distance of the all-purpose town centre (Figure 16). In its way this solution was as dogmatic and inflexible as the neighbourhood unit plan itself. By the 1960s extremist attitudes had been mitigated and more flexible, evolutionary, and pragmatic approaches to residential planning had begun to emerge. It is in the new towns designated during the 1960s that these new attitudes find their fullest expression and where the most important innovations and experiments have been conducted. They are used here to indicate the more recent direction residential planning has taken. Although each new town has its own distinctive

[1] The development of the New Town idea was discussed in Unit 26 and forms a useful background to this section. Mark 1 new towns are those like Harlow or Crawley or Stevenage built in the early postwar years. Mark 2 were Cumbernauld and the abortive Hook project of the 1950s. Mark 3 are the latest new towns designated in the 1960s such as Milton Keynes, Redditch, Telford and Runcorn. The location of the British new towns are shown in Figure 17.

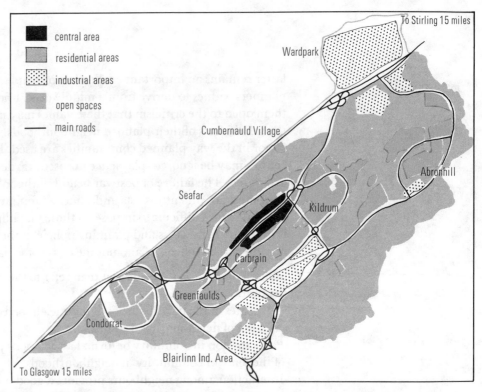

Figure 16 The layout of Cumbernauld   Source: Cumbernauld Development Corporation

Figure 17 New towns in the UK

character and design there are some broad parallels between them. Both differences and similarities may be illustrated by reference to six of the new and expanded town schemes – Milton Keynes, Northampton, Peterborough, Runcorn, Telford, and Washington (for locations see Figure 17).

4.1 New towns: the major planning goals

Most of the modern new town master plans are related to planning goals or objectives. In some plans these are specific goals relating to some aspect of the plan such as the balance of public and private transport, the balance between owner occupied and rented housing, and so on. In other plans the major goals are articulated at the outset and underpin the plan at every stage. Some indication of differences in goal formulation can be gained by comparing the plans. Peterborough's is a very general statement of intent:

... This plan is for people in all their infinite variety of age, need, taste, capacity, and income, and all its objectives amount in sum to a simple aim: to provide for all present and future citizens of Greater Peterborough good homes in safe and pleasant surroundings, a strong economy rich in its diversity of jobs and career opportunities, easily accessible social, professional and commercial services to meet all needs, and generous means for the enjoyment of leisure. (Greater Peterborough Master Plan, p 9)

This could be said of all new towns, and indeed of most new developments. It does not, however, suggest the criteria against which the evolution of the new town may be tested.

Northampton, Telford and Milton Keynes have provided more detailed statements of their goals. The first six of the nine stated objectives of the Northampton plan centre on transport. The remaining three are concerned with the physical form of the town, its population structure and the programming of development. Telford and Milton Keynes are essentially new towns, rather than major expansions of existing large towns as is the case with Peterborough and Northampton. Their planning goals are broadly similar (Figure 18). Both stress the desirability of freedom of choice, of accessibility

Figure 18 The planning goals of Milton Keynes and Telford Sources: Milton Keynes Development Corporation (1970) Vol 1, p 13 and Telford Development Corporation (1969) Vol 1, pp 43–4

Milton Keynes	Telford
1 Opportunity and freedom of choice	1 Freedom of choice
2 Easy movement and access, and good communications	2 Mobility
3 Balance and variety	3 Coherent image and structure
4 An attractive city	4 Realisation of improved living standards
5 Public awareness and participation	5 Flexibility for growth
6 Efficient and imaginative use of resources	6 Maximum use of existing resources

and mobility within the town, of architectural balance and variety, and of the efficient use of resources. Telford also emphasizes the need to build in flexibility as the town develops, and the provision of a viable economic and social infrastructure which will enable the realization of improved living conditions. The Milton Keynes plan lays stress on 'balance and variety' and public participation. While the goal of balance and variety incorporates the provision of adequate social and economic facilities it also encompasses social integration. This, together with the encouragement of public participation in the development of the new town transmits a *social* rather than an *economic* emphasis to the plan. This pervasive social emphasis is very different from that of, say, the Telford plan which is somewhat more technocratic in tone. Whether or not this difference can be expressed in the physical plan is a point of central concern to this unit.

4.2 Physical planning and social consequences

Despite conscious effort to achieve individuality, a striking feature of these new town plans, at least in their residential area planning, is their similarity. Indeed, some elements of Perry's original neighbourhood unit scheme survive in all these plans, although new thinking is also in evidence. There are three elements of residential area planning which we shall consider. These are size, the location of facilities, and the internal layout. The latter two are dealt with together as 'community structure'.

4.2.1 The size of the residential area

In Perry's scheme the size was determined by the catchment area of the elementary (in England and Wales, the primary) school. The school remains an important consideration partly owing to the youthful age structure of most new housing developments and partly through prevailing emphasis on the value of familism. Variations in the structure of the school system result in differences in the size of catchment areas. Size may also be related to the service areas of other local facilities with the result that interpretations vary widely. Runcorn and Telford identify a hierarchy of service provision. The basic units contain about 8,000 people, enough to support at least two 2-form entry or four 1-form entry primary schools (Runcorn) or a middle school (Telford). At Washington the primary school catchment area suggests a unit of about 4,500 population, at Peterborough 4,000 to 5,000 people. Milton Keynes is even more flexible for here the schools and other facilities are not the focus of discrete areas but are distributed throughout the city to enable 'parents to choose between a number of first schools, all available within walking distance of the home'. (Milton Keynes 1970 Vol 1 p 14)

The critical determinant of the size of residential units is the maximum walking distance. This is obviously linked to the provision of first or primary schools, since it is deemed essential for these to be within walking distance of the furthest house within their catchment areas. This maximum distance is regarded as between a quarter and a third of a mile (five to six minutes average walking time). The same principle applies to the location of dwellings relative to other facilities like local shops and bus stops. Variations in gradient or in the age of pedestrians will clearly cause deviations from the average walking time. It is possible to manipulate the densities, layouts, and types of housing to account for such variables. The Runcorn plan describes the balance of forces that has to be struck:

... The size of the communities in terms of population and area has been determined by the economic provision of social facilities related to population and acceptable walking distances to the local centres ... together with a residential density which gives satisfactory housing standards. (Runcorn 1967 p 45)

4.2.2 Community structure

The early new towns stuck fairly rigidly to a set formula with residential areas disposed around a neighbourhood centre comprising schools, shops, pubs, churches and other facilities. Local centres in the middle of residential units are a feature of the Peterborough, Runcorn, Telford and Washington plans. Apart from its obvious economic advantages such an arrangement may also serve a social function. It has 'the advantage of bringing people in the community together at a central point and encourages their social identity' (Runcorn 1967 p 48). Here the idea of promoting social integration within a functional neighbourhood (see Unit 7) in order to develop a sense of community is in evidence.

Milton Keynes offers a radical departure from the centralized residential unit scheme. 'Houses are not grouped to form an inward-looking neighbourhood unit, but will each be part of overlapping catchment areas, according to different functions and the interests and requirements of each household, some within walking distance and some within short car or public transport journeys (Milton Keynes 1970 Vol 1 p 38). The city is being designed as a flexible system in order to meet the planning goals of variety and freedom of choice. Local facilities – bus stops, schools, churches, meeting place, public houses, shops – will be grouped in various combinations, at points where main pedestrian routes cross the main roads (Figure 19). These will form *activity*

Figure 19 Milton Keynes activity centres These are sited at points of intersection between pedestrian walkways and the main roads near the bus stops (Figure 19a). Each centre will have a few activities (Figure 19b) enabling a variety of activities to be within walking distance at different centres (Figure 19c) and more to be within a short bus or car journey (Figure 19d). An activity centre is shown in diagrammatic form in Figure 19e. Source: Milton Keynes Development Corporation (1970) Vol 2, pp 306–7

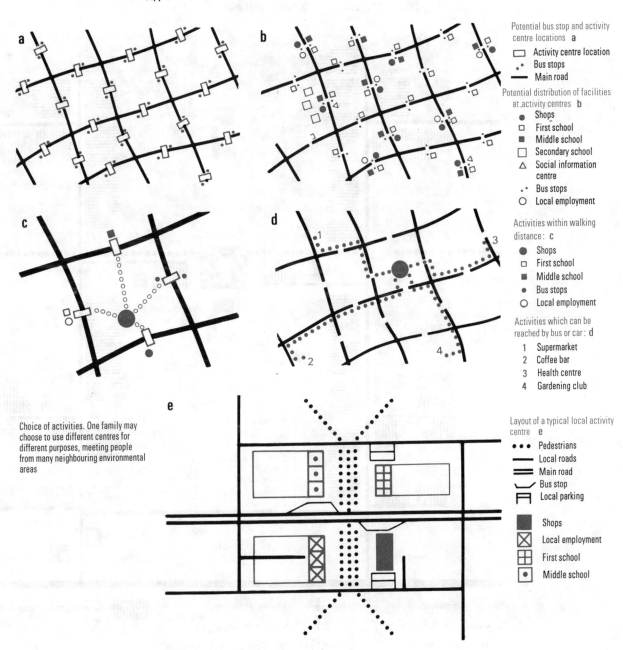

Potential bus stop and activity centre locations a
- ▭ Activity centre location
- · Bus stops
- — Main road

Potential distribution of facilities at activity centres b
- ● Shops
- ◻ First school
- ◼ Middle school
- ☐ Secondary school
- △ Social information centre
- · Bus stops
- ○ Local employment

Activities within walking distance: c
- ● Shops
- ◻ First school
- ◼ Middle school
- • Bus stops
- ○ Local employment

Activities which can be reached by bus or car: d
1. Supermarket
2. Coffee bar
3. Health centre
4. Gardening club

Choice of activities. One family may choose to use different centres for different purposes, meeting people from many neighbouring environmental areas

Layout of a typical local activity centre e
- ••• Pedestrians
- — Local roads
- ═ Main road
- ⌣ Bus stop
- Local parking

- ▮ Shops
- ⊠ Local employment
- ⊞ First school
- ⊡ Middle school

centres and provide the 'threshold' linking the local to the city environment. The hierarchical principle of service provision that remains a feature of most modern plans is here abandoned in favour of 'a continuum of services which ranges from the local to the city-wide' (Milton Keynes 1970 Vol 2 p 310). This approach whereby individuals are offered a range of choices within walking distance and a further range within a short car or bus journey may foster communities of interest as well as communities of residence. It is, of course, too early to say how these ideas will work out in practice. There may, for instance, be a considerable difference in the freedom of choice available to those with cars as opposed to those who must rely on public transport. All we are concerned with here is the impact of defined social goals upon the plan itself.

Elsewhere the more traditional approach of a geographically based community structure has been maintained. At Peterborough and Northampton the plan consists of major residential areas being grafted onto existing towns with a well

Figure 20 Runcorn, diagrammatic community structure   This shows a unit of about 8,000 population divided by the Rapid Transit Route and open space into four neighbourhoods. Source: Runcorn Development Corporation (1967) p 54

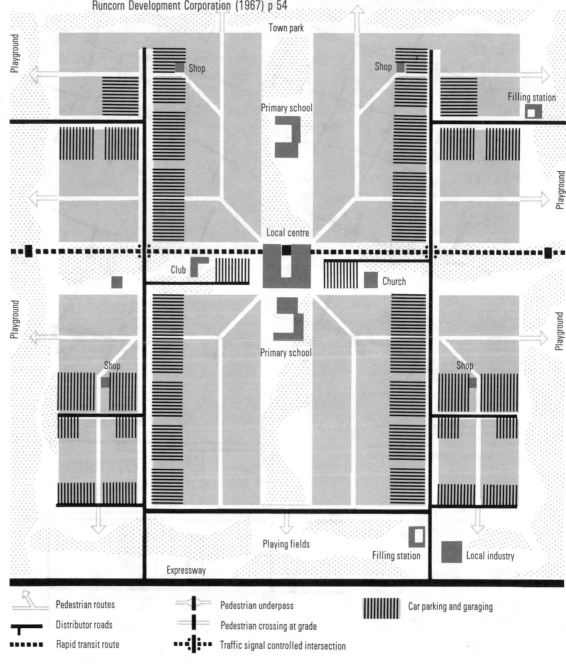

developed range of facilities. Peterborough's expansion takes the form of four townships each between 20,000 and 30,000 divided into identifiable neighbourhoods. Northampton has a similar structure based on service provision and consisting of the town centre, district centres (serving between 25,000 and 50,000 people) and centres within the residential areas. Likewise Washington is compartmentalized into units of about 4,500, groups which are related to local centres with a service radius of two-thirds of a mile. The Washington plan stresses the need for a 'looser and freer structure'. 'The idea of breaking up a town into separate residential areas with fixed boundaries providing a range of services at a certain level for the whole of their population is no longer felt to be socially very relevant' (Washington 1966 p 13). The Washington planners anticipate a trend that reaches its full expression in the Milton Keynes plan prepared by the same consultants.

At Runcorn and Telford the units of 8,000 are subdivided. At Runcorn there are four 'neighbourhoods' physically separated from the others by rapid transit routes, school sites, and open spaces (Figure 20). In Telford the unit is composed of visually defined clusters of about 1,000 people each (Figure 21). In both schemes there are further subdivisions which result in a detailed hierarchy of geographical areas relating the individual to the parts of the city and the city as a whole. The subdivisions within the community groupings are achieved through details of design and layout. There are three common objectives in the design and layout of the residential areas in the new towns under consideration – the provision of a varied, attractive, and traffic-free environment; the organization of buildings and open space in a coherent, intelligible structure; and the attempt to combine privacy with sociability while avoiding conflict.

The first two of these objectives are fairly straightforward. Architectural variation to avoid monotony and to provide visual stimulation was a feature of Perry's plan, and has been an accepted principle since. The Radburn plan was the first systematic effort at pedestrian and vehicle separation though Perry had urged the exclusion of all through traffic from the neighbourhood

Figure 21 Telford, diagrammatic community structure This shows the hierarchical basis of community groupings by which the individual family is related through the dwelling group to the local cluster of about 1,000 population. Eight clusters constitute a community unit of 8,000. These units contain schools and shops within walking distance. Three units make up a district which has senior school facilities, a library, sports centre and a larger shopping centre. Source: Telford Development Corporation (1969)

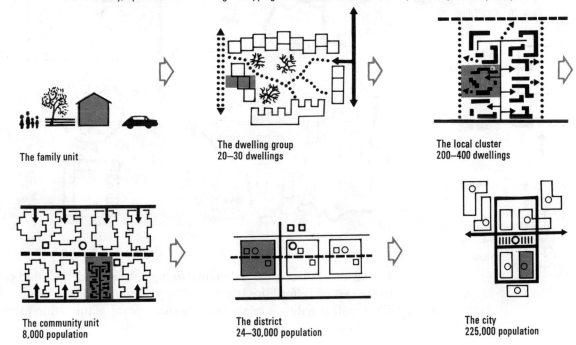

The family unit

The dwelling group
20–30 dwellings

The local cluster
200–400 dwellings

The community unit
8,000 population

The district
24–30,000 population

The city
225,000 population

unit. This principle, too, became firmly established in Britain especially after the publication of the Buchanan Report *Traffic in Towns* in 1963. Buchanan introduced the term 'environmental area' to denote 'an area having no extraneous traffic, and within which considerations of environment predominate over the use of vehicles' (Buchanan 1963 p 252). He insisted that 'no sociological content is implied in this concept – there is no connection with the idea of "neighbourhoods" . . .' (Buchanan 1963, p 63). In each of the six new plans the environmental area principle is adopted and pedestrian walkways are designed as the main means of circulation within the residential areas (Figure 22).

Figure 22 Washington New Town, residential area
22a is an artist's impression of a future residential area as described in the Master Plan
22b shows a residential area when completed Source: Washington Development Corporation

Figure 23 Community structure in Runcorn This diagram illustrates the relationship of the individual to the community in which he lives and which is shown diagrammatically in Figure 20. Source: Runcorn Development Corporation (1967)

Figure 24 Community structure in Washington New Town As in Telford (Figure 21) and Runcorn (Figure 23) Washington has a hierarchical structure relating the individual to the local area and the city as a whole. Source: Washington Development Corporation (1966)

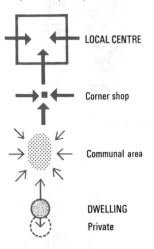
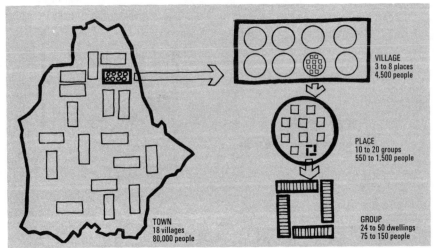

The layout of these areas is designed to suggest visual identity and coherence. In the case of Telford this is achieved by a 'hierarchy of groupings' (Figure 21). The family dwelling is related to a dwelling group of up to thirty dwellings.

This, in turn, forms part of a cluster (200–400 dwellings) about eight of which make up a community unit. In Runcorn (Figure 23) and Peterborough a similar progression is envisaged and Washington relates the *group* (up to fifty dwellings) and the *place* (200 dwellings) with its corner shop, telephone and play area to the village of about 4,500 people (Figure 24). Although there is some similarity in these structures there appears to be no empirical basis for the particular scale chosen for each step in the hierarchy. In all of these residential areas there will be a mixture of dwelling types and sizes but an overall identity will be conferred on them by the use of certain materials or other architectural devices.

4.3 Social integration

In each of these new towns there is some attempt to achieve social integration on a broad scale while maintaining the individual identity of dwelling groups at a small scale. This combination of neighbourhood communities within a socially balanced neighbourhood represents a compromise of postwar residential planning. Within each residential unit there will be a mixture of owner occupied and rented dwellings (the exact proportions depending on the type and rate of population intake and the effect of government policies). Dwelling types and sizes will also be mixed. Thus different income and age groups will be attracted to the same area though the degree of integration will vary. Milton Keynes while accepting that 'some status distinctions will persist in the new city' plans to encourage mixing and to avert any large-scale class-based segregation. The Peterborough plan, while it proposes a similar kind of population mix, gives more emphasis to the preservation of exclusiveness within its residential areas:

... We are all aware that social integration cannot be achieved by indiscriminately mixing up rented housing with privately owned residences. Freedom of choice must include the freedom to choose a congenial social ambience – to live, if one so desires, among people of similar incomes and interests, and to buy, if one values them, seclusion and locational status. (Greater Peterborough Master Plan p 27)

The disposition of rented and private dwellings without stratifying the town on a quasi-class basis is a crucial element in the Runcorn plan. The Northampton plan best expresses the compromise formula that is characteristic of recent approaches to neighbourhood planning:

... A good balance of socio-economic groups both in the town as a whole and in the areas of expansion can avoid some of the limitations of one-class communities. However, this should not suggest enforced social mixing at the local level but rather enclaves of different standards of housing, with wide freedom of choice of size, type and tenure of dwellings; of different densities and standards of privacy. (Northampton 1969 p 19)

With the exception of Milton Keynes none of the plans indicate the possible social consequences of this approach to social integration – rather, it is regarded as a desirable end in itself. They are more explicit on the social effects of grouping dwellings in homogeneous and physically separate groups. This will achieve 'community compatibility and family privacy' (Runcorn); 'the residential seclusion that people apparently desire' (Northampton); 'the formation by residents of a variety of overlapping social relationships' (Washington); or groups where 'neighbourly contact readily occurs' (Telford). The development of a neighbourhood community based on perceived homogeneity is encouraged while the privacy of the individual is respected.

These plans adopt the approach that had been distilled from the experiences of postwar neighbourhood planning. The social values of sense of community and social integration are still present. They are not assumed to be the inevitable outcome of physical planning. The approach, in social terms, is more cautious and passive than was the case in the early postwar years. There is a recognition that current social values vary widely and can only be accommodated within a flexible rather than a rigid planning framework. This aim is expressed in the Telford plan as 'a true reflection of what the planned are seeking in a setting in which known values can be realized collectively and individually' (Telford 1969 p 43).

Only Milton Keynes is distinctively different. Although its social goals are also related to society's values it recognizes that their character and emphasis may change over time. Throughout, the plan is related to 'clear and explicit social goals' which, ultimately, produce a detailed and imaginative appraisal of the social system that is in the process of being created at Milton Keynes. These social goals (Figure 18) are to be achieved through the participation of people in the planning process and through the social development programme. This programme is partly concerned with the social impact of physical planning.

But it also recognizes that many social goals require *social* action for their fulfilment and have little to do with the details of the physical environment. The recognition of the importance of social action is a singular advance in planning thinking. Social development in Milton Keynes will investigate 'the more abstract processes by which societies develop institutional means to secure goals, meet crises, cope with change, and maintain or adopt new life styles' (Milton Keynes 1970 Vol 2 p 119). All new town plans pay attention to the provision of services such as education, health and welfare, shopping, employment and so on. Milton Keynes proposes to go further than this by helping to establish the means by which individuals can respond to the challenges and opportunities afforded by their new environment. This aspect of the plan is unique in that this role has not previously been an integral part of the planning process, unusual in that its scope and method of operation is largely undefined, and original in that it introduces a wholly new and necessary dimension into the concept of social planning. We must await the evidence of what happens in practice.

4.4 Residential planning in established towns

Neighbourhood planning in new towns is rather a special case. In them land is wholly controlled by a development corporation and the planners are largely responsible for the phasing, design and layout of new developments. In the more typical situation of an established town or city, land is held by the local authorities, developers and private individuals. Planning residential areas tends to be an activity often restricted to relatively small developments. Whereas new town planners can fit comprehensive local area plans into the scheme for the town as a whole, planners in established towns must work within the constraints of the existing built environment. Although the pace and direction of urban development is controlled by the planning authority there are many constraints which must be taken into consideration. These include the relationship of the development to the existing urban pattern, the availability of services, the acquisition of the land, and so on. Local authorities are also able to act as estate developers and to keep a fairly tight control over the layout and density of housing on land allocated to private builders. Where land is bought by small builders detailed design is, within limits, the responsibility of the individual builder. Less control is likely to be exercised over large developers whose standards are, nevertheless, often high. A further factor is the

Figure 25 Development of residential areas in established towns
On the urban fringe land is allocated to builders (a). Small builders (b) develop their land according to a plan designed by the local authority (c), whereas large builders may be responsible for the design of a complete estate (d). Once developed these areas may incorporate high density pedestrian layouts (e) and individually designed houses in more conventional layouts (f). Council housing may also be mixed in with the private developments (g).

need to accommodate local authority building programmes from time to time. The outcome is a residential area that is a patchwork of small developments which the planning authority may attempt to weld into a coherent and functionally self-contained residential area. A conscious exposition of the social goals of planning is nearly always absent in such residential areas. Given the organic and piecemeal way in which they tend to grow, and the consequent task of planning a comprehensive framework for development this is not surprising. But social planning is no less necessary in established settlements than it is in new towns.

SAQ 4 Comment on the following statements and then refer to the comments given at the end of the unit.

a The neighbourhood unit concept has little relevance to the planning of residential areas in the latest British new towns.

b Neighbourhoods in the early British new towns were conceived as communities, those in the latest new towns are based on the provision of services.

c In most of the recent new towns the goal of social integration is pursued at the neighbourhood level.

d The social planning goals of the latest British new towns are related to a physical planning framework.

5 Conclusion
5.1 Planners, social scientists, goals and values

Planning residential areas has been used to illustrate three themes related to the social functions of planners. Certain conclusions have been reached for each of these themes:

1 *The relationship between planners and social scientists*. There has developed a greater degree of mutual awareness and co-operation between social scientists and planners since the era when the neighbourhood unit idea was first introduced. Although this interaction has been fitful, the fruits of it are becoming apparent in plans such as that for Milton Keynes. The social scientist is beginning to fulfil a number of functions – as source of information, as critic, as evaluator – which enable him to participate at all stages in the evolution of a plan. As Leo Kuper put it in 1951:

... The task of the social scientist is to unmask the values and assumptions, to trace their derivation and point out ambiguities; to analyse on purely logical grounds, the rationality of the conclusions drawn from these assumptions and value judgements; and to enquire into the compatibility of ends, as for example, whether the strengthening of neighbourhood spirit might not weaken the sense of a wider civic entity. (Kuper 1951 p 243)

Planning in many places is still approached from a technological and physical rather than from a social viewpoint so the 'revolution' is by no means completed.

2 *The social and physical goals of planning*. Not only were certain physical and social goals incompatible within the framework of the neighbourhood unit plan but the social goals themselves were mutually contradictory. A simple causal relationship between environment and social behaviour does not exist. The neighbourhood unit was found to be larger than the neighbourhood community. Social integration tended to foster rather than reduce social segregation. Once the irreconcilability of certain social and physical planning goals was recognized a reaction against neighbourhood planning set in. This reaction has now been succeeded by a more cautious approach characterized by an awareness of social processes that may or may not be related to the physical environment.

3 *Societal and planning values*. Although it is widely acknowledged that planning modifies rather than controls social change, the importance of values should not be underestimated. In the heyday of neighbourhood unit planning the question of values was rarely raised though the divergent values of the planners and of the planned was sometimes visually evident in the way the new neighbourhoods were treated. Such a manifest conflict had a positive result for it forced planners to consider their original assumptions. In a situation of greater self-awareness where planners seek to represent the values of society at large the question arises – whose values? Inevitably planners will attempt to represent what is presumed to be the consensus, a consensus that is in fact imbued with middle class values. This position confers upon them a certain amount of freedom to experiment and this accounts for the differences in the new town plans. But this freedom is confined to a mild liberalism on the one hand and a moderate conservatism on the other, both of which tend to sustain the *status quo*. The more extreme positions which, in terms of residential planning could, perhaps, result in complete socio-economic and racial segregation at the reactionary end or total social integration on the radical side, are unlikely to be promoted in a society like Britain which responds intuitively to consensus values.

5.2 Planners, people and conflict

Finally we can consider neighbourhood planning as part of the broader issue of planners and the people for whom they plan. The neighbourhood provides an interesting example of a concept that became value-laden and which has been the subject of different interpretations in the planning field. The neighbourhood unit idea nicely illustrates the relationship between planning and social science. But since it is concerned with a future and not a present population it tells us little of the relationship between planners and the planned. Neighbourhood planning is broad in its scope and its impact is rarely immediate or intrusive. The same cannot be said of transportation planning, of urban renewal and redevelopment where disruption is often caused which brings the authorities into confrontation with the people directly affected. This raises questions of public participation, pressure group politics, and community action, issues which have not been looked at in this unit (see Unit 22).

These localized conflicts are symptomatic of a more general conflict. It is often conceptualized as bureaucracy versus the individual, or simply 'Us' versus 'Them'. But this is an oversimplification. Planners, or rather the politicians whom they serve, must frequently exercise choices which involve the distribution of resources among different groups in the population (see Harvey in Stewart 1972). Urban renewal may benefit the relatively well off, who can afford the rents of city centre redevelopment schemes, or in the case of public housing schemes, those able to secure a tenancy. The cost of such renewal will fall most heavily on the former inhabitants who found cheap accommodation and a sense of community in the area. Similarly, the construction of urban motorways represents some redistribution of resources from public to private transport. Such motorways impose heavy costs on the areas through which they pass and pre-empt resources from other projects. Other examples, such as the siting of shopping centres or the provision of recreational facilities, raise similar issues.

Gans argues that, for various reasons, there is a tendency for private enterprise to allocate in favour of the affluent. He suggests that 'the government policies with which the planner is concerned ought to be *compensatory*' (Gans in Stewart 1972 p 382). In Britain there are examples of deliberate attempts to divert resources to underprivileged areas (eg educationally deprived areas). But these attack the symptoms, not the cause of the problem, which is poverty. The concentration of the symptoms of social malaise – crime and delinquency, broken families, substandard housing, poor health and education – in certain inner urban areas is a reflection of fundamental economic and social inequalities.

Until recently, underprivileged neighbourhoods have been passive recipients of various forms of subsidy. There are signs, especially in the USA, that they are becoming more organized and their demands for an improved environment more insistent. In middle class neighbourhoods there is a tradition of organized response to specific threats. In deprived neighbourhoods people are becoming more aware of their potential political power.

It is this kind of pressure that is likely to change the direction of all forms of planning. Hitherto the focus has been on the provision of a satisfactory built environment and the social and economic infrastructure for a stable community. In future, the emphasis may be more on the means of overcoming problems of poverty in order to reduce the conflict that stems from it. In Gans's words 'we should concentrate on the people and on the social and economic forces which foster their deprivation rather than on neighbourhood conditions which are themselves consequences of those forces' (Gans 1964). The idea of a neighbourhood as a free-standing sub-community within the city is a very partial one (Boal 1972) and may be irrelevant to planning needs. Increasing mobility and affluence are leading to a demand for freedom of choice which cannot be attained within a circumscribed neighbourhood. At the same time the poorer sections of the community, who are immobile and therefore more dependent on the locality, make demands upon their neighbourhood that cannot always be met by conventional planning techniques. Residential area planning was for long confined to the manipulation of physical variables within a defined area. Increasingly it is being regarded in the much wider context of a dynamic social environment in which change is conditioned by social rather than physical processes.

Planning must adapt to the changing needs and aspirations of the society it serves. Where there is conflict it is not easy to evaluate opposing demands. Planning is neither remote nor objective but a process that demands involvement and that requires a degree of commitment. The environment most of us inhabit today is the product of past attitudes to planning. Tomorrow's environment depends upon decisions being taken now. What sort of environment that will be is the subject of the final block of this course.

SAQ 5 Comment on the following statements:
a Both planners and social scientists attempt to reflect the values of society.
b Focus on the planning at the neighbourhood level may hinder the achievement of the broader social goals of planning.

SAQ 6 The following questions are based on the two articles in Stewart (1972) that are required reading for this unit.
1 According to Rein, there are four sources of authority through which planners may justify their intervention. These are the authorities of (i) expertise, (ii) bureaucratic position, (iii) consumer preferences and (iv) professional values. Which source of authority would a planner be most likely to invoke in the following cases?
a When seeking to persuade politicians in favour of a particular road project on grounds of its economic viability.
b When trying to prevent the clearance of a particular neighbourhood.
c When attempting to change the existing social structure by working through the established institutions.

d   When attempting to change the existing social structure by challenging the existing institutions.

2 According to Rein there are three strategies which planners can adopt in order to secure the objectives of intervention. They are (i) elite consensus, (ii) rational analysis, and (iii) citizen participation. With which of these strategies would you associate the following objectives:

a   To arouse and sustain public interest.

b   To achieve reform while operating within the existing institutional framework.

c   To select a problem for systematic investigation.

d   To reconcile conflicts of values between various groups in society.

3 In *Planning for People, Not Buildings*, Gans:

a   argues from a middle class viewpoint.

b   argues against a middle class viewpoint.

c   is concerned with the social reforms that may be encouraged through the planning process.

d   advocates greater emphasis on the social aspects of physical planning.

Which of the above statements do you think are substantially correct?

Comments on SAQs

Comments SAQ 1   *Statement a* is broadly true although there is increasing evidence of a change in attitude on the part of both planners and social scientists. Planners have, on the whole, been concerned with the efficient organization of the built environment and have applied specific standards of space, services and amenity in housing developments. Social scientists have criticized planners for failing to accommodate social processes in their plans. Part of the reason for this lies in the failure of social scientists to provide any practical interpretations of their findings. There is, as a result, a barrier to communication between planners and social scientists (*Statement b*) though there are signs of increasing cooperation between them and the development of a more integrated approach to social planning is beginning to emerge.

These differences in approach are evident at the level of neighbourhood planning (*Statement c*). Neighbourhood possesses both a social and a spatial dimension (see Unit 7). Planners are more concerned with the spatial aspects which can be expressed in physical terms. Social scientists (mainly sociologists) concentrate on the social dimension of the neighbourhood as a localized community of social interaction (*Statement d*).

Comments SAQ 2   *Statement a.* The concept of social balance at the neighbourhood level is the antithesis of the spatial segregation on socio-economic lines that is so prevalent in Western cities. It was at one time felt that social balance could be the means for encouraging social interaction between the different classes. There was also an element of social reform in the idea since it was thought that the leadership and social control exercised by the educated and wealthy would improve the standards of the working classes. Later (as we shall see) the emphasis shifted towards more egalitarian principles and social balance came to be regarded as a means for reducing segregation (see SAQ 3e).

Statement b. Perry was primarily concerned with the physical planning principles necessary to ensure a good living environment though he assumed that his plan would encourage neighbourliness. He did not consider the other social goals (sense of community, social integration) in residential planning that later became one of the major reasons for the scheme's enthusiastic adoption by some sociologists and planners (*Statement c*).

Statement d. British interpretations of the neighbourhood scheme varied. Although the school catchment area was the basis of most schemes they differed in certain important respects from Perry's original plan (eg in the location of services, notably shops at the centre of each neighbourhood rather than at road junctions between them). The neighbourhood unit was applied in Britain as a detailed physical plan giving an optimal arrangement of housing and other facilities rather than as a set of social planning principles.

Comments SAQ 3 *Statement a.* It is unlikely that the early advocates of neighbourhood units thought of them in a sociological sense as localized networks of neighbourly interaction (see Unit 7). However, they undoubtedly believed the neighbourhood unit would recreate in an urban setting the primary close-knit community (*gemeinschaft*) associated with village life. In reality the urban neighbourhood constitutes a more 'open' society than the village.

Statement b. Participation in formal associations does not provide an adequate basis for measuring the somewhat elusive concept of sense of community. Participation varies according to socio-economic characteristics but it does seem to be important in enabling people to initiate the more intimate primary relationships characteristic of a community neighbourhood. But once this intimacy has been achieved participation tends to decline except among the socially mobile. In general, increasing participation in formal associations appears to *substitute* for the development of informal primary relationships.

Statement c. Neighbourly interaction is clearly important but other forms of interaction especially among kin may play a greater part in the development of a sense of community. The sense of community is greater where people share similar characteristics, notably of class or stage in the family life cycle (*Statement d*).

Statement e. SAQ2a suggested that the social goals of neighbourhood planning derive from egalitarian principles. It is agreed that by integrating different social and economic groups within the same neighbourhood, barriers of class and income will be reduced. Quite how this would be achieved without more fundamental changes in society was never made explicit.

Statement f. The goal of social integration requires a socially balanced population, whereas the goal of sense of community is best satisfied by a homogeneous population. The two goals are mutually exclusive and cannot be secured simultaneously within the same neighbourhood. It is possible, however, through the process of housing allocation and through careful design to achieve social balance over the neighbourhood as a whole while at the same time dividing it up into small but relatively homogeneous housing units (*Statement g*).

Comments SAQ 4 *Statement a.* Planning residential areas in the latest new towns tends to be more flexible than in the earlier ones and the conscious application of the neighbour-hood unit concept has been wholly abandoned. Nevertheless, some of Perry's principles remain in many of the latest schemes.

Statement b. Although this is probably true the planning outcome has often been similar, at least in terms of community structure. In all the British new towns residential areas are designed as discrete, spatially bound units focusing around particular services. Milton Keynes, in contrast, has abandoned this approach in favour of a more flexible system of overlapping service areas.

Statement c. In all the latest new towns a balanced intake of population is assumed (though in practice the composition tends to vary according to the stage of development and changes in housing and employment policies). Most of the plans recognize that while integration may be achieved over the town as a whole, at the local level the segregation of people in the public and private housing sectors is acceptable.

Statement d. In the later new town schemes the emphasis tends to be upon the physical aspects of layout and design in residential areas. Physical planning is regarded as a means for encouraging the satisfaction of social goals rather than as a method for determining them. Milton Keynes is again exceptional in that its plan recognizes that many social goals are unrelated to physical planning and require social measures for their fulfilment.

Comments SAQ 5
Statement a. Few values are held in common by society as a whole. Both planners and social scientists tend to reflect particular sets of values, usually those of the middle class, which they interpret as the consensus viewpoint. In cases where these values are not shared by those for whom they plan, conflicts of interest may arise. The role of values in the planning process is a central theme of the articles by Gans and Rein in Stewart.

Statement b. This is especially likely where the emphasis is upon physical planning at the neighbourhood level. In any case it is unlikely that the social goals of neighbourhood planning, notably social integration, can be achieved without fundamental changes at the level of society. Certain social problems may be localized in particular neighbourhoods but their solution lies, not in physical planning at the local level, but in the reduction of inequalities in society itself.

Comments SAQ 6
1a   Usually the planner would employ his expertise in his role as a bureaucrat to persuade politicians and so (i) and (ii) are most likely. It is, of course, possible that he would act on behalf of clients or that his own values suggest an alternative course of action and so (iii) and (iv) may play a part in determining his attitude to a particular scheme.

1b   (iii) seems most likely in this case but the others, especially (iv), are quite possible.

1c   (ii) is most likely.

1d   (iii) is most likely though he may be influenced by the values of, at least, some of his profession (iv).

You will notice that none of the above are mutually exclusive. They tend to differ in emphasis. Thus (i) and (ii) tend to represent existing established sources of authority whereas (iii) and (iv) represent the sources that challenge the establishment.

2a   (iii).

2b   (i).

2c   (ii).

2d   Mainly (i). Rational analysis (ii) is not supposedly concerned with values and citizen participation (iii) implies some conflict of values, the reconciliation of which is, presumably, a task for the established political process (i).

3a   Gans attempts to lay bare the conflicts that arise when a middle class viewpoint is imposed upon those who do not share it. In this sense he is arguing against the middle class viewpoint (b), though, he is clearly addressing himself to a middle class audience which, he anticipates, may share his liberal reformist attitudes (c). He stresses the need for more emphasis on the social aspects of physical planning but acknowledges that many social goals lie outside the influence of physical planning (d).

References ABERCROMBIE, P. (1944) *Greater London Plan*, London, HMSO.

AXELROD, M. (1956) 'Urban Structure and Social Participation' in *American Sociological Review*, 21, February, pp 13–18.

BARNETT, DAME HENRIETTA (1921) *Canon Barnett, His Life, Work, and Friends*, London, John Murray.

BELL, C. and NEWBY, H. (1972) *Community Studies*, London, George Allen and Unwin.

BELL, W. and BOAT, MARION D. (1957) 'Urban Neighbourhoods and Informal Social Relations' in *American Journal of Sociology*, 62, January, pp 391–8.

BELL, W. and FORCE, MARYANNE T. (1956) 'Urban Neighbourhood Types and Participation in Formal Associations' in *American Sociological Review*, 21, pp 26–34.

BLOWERS, A. T. (1970) 'Council Housing: The Social Implications of Layout and Design in an Urban Fringe Estate' in *Town Planning Review*, 41, 1, January, pp 80–92.

BLOWERS, A. T. (1973) 'London's out-county estates: A reappraisal', in *Town and Country Planning*, September.

BLOWERS, A. T., HAMNETT, C. R. and SARRE, P. V. (eds) (1974) *The Future of Cities*, London, Hutchinson Educational (the Reader).

BLUMENFELD, H. (1971) *The Modern Metropolis*, Cambridge, Mass, MIT Press (set book).

BOAL, F. W. (1972) 'The Urban Residential Sub-community – A Conflict Interpretation', in *Area*, 4, 3, pp 164–8.

BUCHANAN REPORT (1963) *Traffic in Towns*, London, HMSO (shortened edition, Penguin Books, 1964).

BUTTIMER, ANNE (1971) 'Sociology and Planning' in *Town Planning Review*, 42, 2, April, pp 145–80; shortened article in STEWART, M. (ed) (1972) (set book).

COLLISON, P. (1954) 'Town Planning and the Neighbourhood Unit Concept' in *Public Administration*, 32.

COOLEY, C. H. (1909) *Social Organization* (new ed 1972), New York, Scribners.

DAHIR, J. (1947) *The Neighbourhood Unit Plan: Its Spread and Acceptance*, New York, The Russell Sage Foundation.

DENNIS, N. (1958) 'The Popularity of the Neighbourhood Community Idea' in *Sociological Review*, 6, 2, pp 199–206; also in PAHL, R. E. (ed) (1968) (set book).

DEUTSCH, M. and COLLINS, MARY E. (1955) 'Interracial Housings' in MAYER, R. R. (1972) pp 46–52.

DEWEY, R. (1950) 'The Neighbourhood, Urban Ecology, and City Planners' in *Americal Sociological Review*, 15, August, pp 502–7; also in HATT, P. K. and REISS, A. J. JR (1951) pp 783–90.

DUDLEY REPORT (1944) *The Design of Dwellings*, London, HMSO.

GANS, H. J. (1961) 'The Balanced Community: Homogeneity or Heterogeneity in Residential Areas?' in *Journal of the American Institute of Planners*, 27, 3, August, pp 176–84; also in GANS, H. J. (1972) pp 140–59.

GANS, H. J. (1964) *Social and Physical Planning for the Elimination of Urban Poverty* in ROSENBERG, B., GERVER, I. and HOWTON, W. (eds) (1964) *Mass Society in Crisis: Social Problems and Social Pathology*, New York, Macmillan, pp 629–44.

GANS, H. J. (1969) 'Planning for People, not Buildings' in *Environment and Planning*, 1, pp 33–46; also in STEWART, M. (ed) (1972) pp 363–84 (set book).

GANS, H. J. (1972) *People and Plans*, London, Penguin Books.

GIBBERD, SIR F. (1968) *The development of Harlow New Town*, Alcan: Universities Conference Programme, 3 April 1968.

GOSS, A. (1961) 'Neighbourhood Units in British New Towns' in *Town Planning Review*, 32, 1, April, pp 66–82.

HARVEY, D. (1971) 'Social processes, spatial form and the redistribution of real income in an urban system' in STEWART, M. (ed) (1972) (set book).

HATT, P. K. and REISS, A. J. JR (1951) *Cities and Society*, New York, The Free Press.

HERAUD, B. J. (1968) 'Social Class and the New Towns' in *Urban Studies*, 5, 1, February, pp 33–58.

HOWARD, E. (1902) *Garden Cities of Tomorrow*, also in Faber Books, 1965.

KELLER, SUZANNE (1966) 'Social Class in Physical Planning' in *International Social Sciences Journal*, 18, 4.

KELLER, SUZANNE (1968) *The urban neighbourhood: a sociological perspective*, New York, Random House.

KUPER, L. (1951) 'Social Science Research and the Planning of Urban Neighbourhoods' in *Social Forces*, 39, 3, March, pp 237–43.

KUPER, L. (ed) (1953) 'Blueprint for Living Together' in *Living in Towns*, Cresset Press, pp 1–203.

LITWAK, E. (1961) 'Voluntary Association and Neighbourhood Cohesion' in *American Sociological Review*, 26, pp 258–71.

LONDON COUNTY COUNCIL (1949) *Post-war Housing 1945–9*, London, LCC.

LONDON COUNTY COUNCIL (1943) *County of London Plan*, prepared for the LCC by J. H. FORSHAW, and PATRICK ABERCROMBIE, London, Macmillan.

LOCK, M., GROVE, D. and KING, G. (1952) *Bedford by the River*, London, John Murray.

MANN, P. H. (1958) 'The Socially Balanced Neighbourhood Unit' in *Town Planning Review*, 29, 2, July, pp 91–8.

MAYER, R. R. (1972) *Social Planning and Social Change*, Englewood Cliffs, NJ, Prentice-Hall.

MCCONNELL, S. B. (1959) 'The Neighbourhood' in *Community Planning*, 9, 3, September.

MERTON, R. K. (1951) 'The Social Psychology of Housing' in *Current Trends in Social Psychology*, University of Pittsburgh Press, pp 163–217.

MILTON KEYNES DEVELOPMENT CORPORATION (1970) *The Plan for Milton Keynes*, Vols 1 and 2, Report by Llewelyn-Davies, Weeks, Forestier-Walker and Bor, Milton Keynes Development Corporation.

MUMFORD, C. (1954) 'The Neighbourhood and the Neighbourhood Unit Concept' in *Town Planning Review*, 24, 4, January.

NEW TOWNS COMMISSION (1946) *Final Report*, London, HMSO.

NORTHAMPTON DEVELOPMENT CORPORATION (1969) *Northampton Master Plan*, Report by HUGH WILSON and LEWIS WOMERSLEY, Northampton Development Corporation.

OSBORN, F. J. and WHITTICK, A. (1963) *New Towns*, London, Leonard Hill.

PAHL, R. E. (ed) (1968) *Readings in Urban Sociology*, Oxford, Pergamon Press (set book).

PERRY, C. A. (1929) 'The Neighbourhood Unit, a Scheme of Arrangement for the Family-Life Community' in *The Regional Survey of New York and its Environs*, Vol 7, New York, pp 22–140.

PERRY, C. A. (1939) *Housing for the Machine Age*, New York, The Russell Sage Foundation.

PETERBOROUGH DEVELOPMENT CORPORATION, *Greater Peterborough Master Plan*, Peterborough Development Corporation.

PEP (POLITICAL AND ECONOMIC PLANNING) (1949) 'Can Communities be Planned?' in *Planning*, 15, 296, 28 March, pp 259–78.

RIEMER, S. (1951) 'Villages in Metropolis' in *British Journal of Sociology*, 2, March, pp 31–43.

ROSENBERG, M. (1965) 'Society and the Adolescent Self-Image' in MAYER, R. R. (1972) pp 58–65.

ROSOW, I. (1967) 'Social Integration of the Aged' in MAYER, R. R. (1972) pp 52–8.

RUNCORN DEVELOPMENT CORPORATION (1967) *Runcorn New Town*, Report by Arthur Ling and Associates, Runcorn Development Corporation.

SHEVKY, E. and BELL, W. (1955) *Social Area Analysis in Theory, Illustrative Application and Computational Procedures*, Palo Alto, Stanford University Press.

STEWART, M. (ed) (1972) *The City: Problems of planning*; Harmondsworth, Penguin (set book).

TELFORD DEVELOPMENT CORPORATION (1969) *Telford Development Proposals*, Vols 1 and 2, Report by John Madin Design Group, Telford Development Corporation.

TETLOW, J. D. (1959) 'Sources of the Neighbourhood Idea' in *Journal of the Town Planning Institute*, April.

WALDORF, D. (1967) 'Neighbourhood Unit Assessments – Simple or Complex?' in *Official Architecture and Planning*, March, pp 372–7.

WASHINGTON DEVELOPMENT CORPORATION (1966) *Washington New Town Master Plan and Report*, Report by Llewelyn-Davies, Weeks and Partners, Washington Development Corporation.

WHITE, L. E. (1950) *Community or Chaos: New Housing Estates and their Social Problems*, London, National Council of Social Service.

WILLMOTT, P. (1962) 'Housing Density and Town Design in a New Town: A Pilot Study at Stevenage' in *Town Planning Review*, 33, 2, July, pp 115–27.

YOUNG, M. and WILLMOTT, P. (1957) *Family and Kinship in East London*, London, Routledge and Kegan Paul, also in Penguin Books, 1962.

Acknowledgements

Grateful acknowledgement is made to the following sources for material used in this unit:

Figure 1: The Yorkshire Post; *Figure 2:* Faber and Faber Limited, and the MIT Press, Cambridge, Massachusetts for E. Howard, *Garden Cities of Tomorrow*; *Figure 3:* Regional Plan Association for C. Perry in *Regional Survey of New York and its Environs*, 7; *Figure 4:* the author and the Estates Gazette Ltd for L. B. Keeble, 'Principles and practice of town and country planning'; *Figure 5:* Aerofilms Ltd; *Figure 10:* The American Sociological Association and the author for E. Litwak, 'Voluntary association and neighbourhood cohesion' in *American Sociological Review*, 26, 1961; *Figure 16:* Cumbernauld Development Corporation; *Figure 18:* Milton Keynes Development Corporation and Telford Development Corporation; *Figure 19:* Milton Keynes Development Corporation and Messrs Llewelyn-Davies Weeks Forestier-Walker & Bor; *Figures 20 and 23:* Runcorn Development Corporation; *Figure 21:* Telford Development Corporation for *Telford Development Proposals*, 1, 1969; *Figures 22 and 24:* Washington Development Corporation; *Table 1:* The American Sociological Association and the authors for W. Bell and M. T. Force, 'Urban neighbourhood types and participation in formal associations' in *American Sociological Review*, 21; *Tables 2 and 3:* Longman Group Journals Division and the author for B. J. Heraud, 'Social class and the new towns' in *Urban Studies*, 5, 1.

Urban development